Your Personal Guide to Hajj Umrah Ziyarat

Author(s):

Mahmud & Zehra Habib [3]

Useful guide for those making pilgrimage. Includes suggestions for books, hotels, flights, transportation, visa, as well as a health guide, maps, laws and practices, supplications and salutations, information about cities, and even a shopping guide.

Category:

Hajj (Pilgrimage) [4]

Topic Tags:

Pilgrimage [5]
Laws [6]
information [7]

Introduction

In the Name of Allah, the Most Beneficent, the Most Merciful.

By the grace of the Almighty Allah (SWT), we indeed have been blessed with the honour of compiling this booklet for the benefit of those going to Umrah, Hajj and/or Ziyarat of the Fourteen Masoomeen A.S.

Our first calling for Hajj was in 1983 and since then, we have been invited back for Hajj and Hajj Umrah over 17 times over the past sixteen (16) years. We have also had the pleasure of serving thousands of Momineen and Mominaat, including residents of Canada, United States, Jamaica, Britain, Australia, Sweden and Germany.

This booklet was designed to provide you with some insight and clarification as you embark on your spiritual journey.

We sincerely hope this booklet proves to be useful and we ask that you pass it on to others who,

Inshallah, will be fortunate enough to go also.

We are planning, Inshallah, to reproduce the booklet periodically so you are requested to advise us of any errors and omissions.

Please remember us in your prayers.

Wa'Salaam

**Mahmud & Zehra Habib
Organizer**

Toronto, Canada - March, 1998/Dhul-qa'dah 1418

Recommended Books

• **Hajj**

By Dr. Ali Shariati

• **Hajj Manasek**

According to the Fatwa of:
Ayatullah al-Odhma – Sayyid Ali Husayni Seestani
Translated by Hajj Mortaza Lakaha
Reviewed by: Ayatullah Dr. Seyed Fadhel Milani

• **Adabul Haramain**

By Sayyid Jawad Husayny Shaharudy

• **Rahnuma al-Hujjaj**

According to the Fatwa of:
Marhoom Ayatullah Abul Qasim El-Khouei
Compiled by Hujjatul Islam Wal-Moslemeen
Alhaj Seyed Ali Abid Rizvi

• **Pilgrims' Guide: Selected Supplications**

Translated by Dr. Liyakatali Takim

• **Mafatih-ul-Jinaan**

• **Tofatul-Zaireen**

• **Ziyarat – of the 14 Masoomeen**

Compiled and written
By Hadi Husayn Sayyid
Printed by Peermohamed Ibrahim Trust, Karachi.

All above books are available from:
Mehrab Publishers & Distributors (Canada)
17 Kevi Crescent, Richmond Hill, Ontario L4B 3C8
Telephone # (905) 731-6920
Fax number (905) 886-3430
E-mail: devji@ican.net [8]

Hotels

In Saudi Arabia, Jordon, Syria, Iran & Iraq

Saudi Arabia – Jeddah

Albilad Hotel Movenpick, a five Star Hotel on the Cornish Drive, excellent dining room with open buffet. Fax # 011-966-2-654-7098.

Sheraton Hotel, a five Star Hotel on the Cornish Drive, excellent dining room with open buffet. Fax # 011-966-2-699-2660

Helnan Red Sea Palace Hotel, a five 5 Star Hotel at the City Centre (Balad), excellent dining room with open buffet. Fax # 011-966-2-642-2395.

Medina Munawara

Sheraton Hotel, a five star Hotel - 7 km from the Holy Haram – excellent dinning room with open buffet, shuttle service and a rest house near available for the use by Hujjaj near the Holy Haram, Fax # 011-966-4-846-0385.

Medina Oberoi, a five star hotel - two minute walk to Masjid al-Nabawee, Medina. Fax #011-966-4-826-3155.

Green Palace Hotel - a four star hotel - four minute walk to the Holy Haram. Fax # 011-966-4--24-2666

Al Attas Hotel – a three star hotel – a minute walk to the Holy Haram. Fax # 011-966-4-8233-0285.

Madinah Reem Hotel - a four star hotel - 3 minute to the Holy Haram - The Masjid al-Nabi as well as Jannatul-Baquee can easily be viewed Fax # 011-966-4-825-5725

Makkah

Hilton Towers - a five star hotel; a minute walk to the Holy Haram, Fax # 011-966-2-537-6500.

Kindah Palace - a five star hotel, two minute walk to the Holy Haram, Fax 011-966-2-574-3535.

Ajyad Makkah Hotel - a five star hotel, six minutes walk to the Holy Haram. Shuttle bus service available – excellent dining room buffet style. Fax # 011-966-2-574-6061.

Syria

Damascus

Ebla Cham Palace - a five star de-luxe hotel with excellent dining room with open buffet. It is about 15 minutes drive to Bibi Zainab AS's Raudhah.
Fax # 011-963-11-223-4805.

Other Five Stars Hotels

Semiramis - Meridien - Sheraton
Cham Palace

Jordan

Amman

Five star hotels
Intercontinental - Forte Grand - Marriot
Rooms are with attached English Style bathrooms.

Al-Quds

Jerusalem – West Bank

The Seven Arches – a four star hotel.

Islamic Republic of Iran

Tehran

Azadi International Hotel - a five star hotel - rooms with attached English style bathrooms. Excellent dining room with open buffet, Fax # 011-98-21-2073038.

Homa Hotel - a five star hotel - Rooms with attached English style bathrooms. Excellent dining room with open buffet. Fax # 011-98-21-8773021.

Mashad

Laleh Hotel - a five star hotel - acceptable dining room with open buffet. Telephone #011-98--1-894845, 9 lines. Few rooms with attached English style toilets.

Homa Hotel, a five star hotel - Rooms with attached English Style bathrooms. Excellent dinning room with open buffet.

Republic of Iraq

Bagdaad

Al-Rashid Hotel - a five star hotel - Rooms with attached English Style bathrooms. Acceptable dining room with limited menu.

Sheraton Hotel - four star hotel - Rooms with attached English Style bathrooms. Acceptable dining room with limited menu.

Karbala'

Makki's Rest House - to be considered as two Star guesthouse across Hazrat Abbas A.S. Raudhah; few rooms with attached English Style bathrooms.

Hotel Zainabiya - a two star hotel few kilometers away from the Holy Haram. You need a bus to visit the Holy Haram.

There are many new hotels in Karbala' but their standards are low and to be standard considered as two star hotel. Most of them do not have English Style Bathrooms.

Najaf

The only popular hotel is Zam Zam Hotel, again to be considered as a 2 star hotel. Only a few rooms have attached English Style bathrooms.

Embassies for Visas

Saudi Arabia

The Kingdom of Saudi Arabia for Hajj & Umra Visa.

In Canada

The Consular Section, 99 Bank Street, Suite # 260, Ottawa, Ont. K1P 6B9, telephone # (613) 237-4100 Fax # (613) 237-0567

In the United States

New York, The Consular Section
866 United Nations Plaza, Room # 480, New York, NY 10017, Telephone # (212) 752-2740.

Washington. The Consular Section
601 Newhamshire Avenue North W., Washington DC 20037, Telephone # (202) 342-3800.

Houston. The Consular Section
5718 Westheimer, Suite # 1500, Houston, TX 77057, Telephone # (713) 785-5577.

Los Angeles. The Consular Section
10900 Wilshire Blvd., Suite # 830, Los Angeles, CA 90024, Telephone # (310) 208-6566.

Jordan

The Hashemite Kingdom of Jordan

In Canada

100 Bronson Avenue, Suite # 701, Ottawa KAR 6G8
Telephone # (613) 238-8090

Syria

The Embassy of The Syrian Arab Republic

In Canada

111 St. Urban, Suite # R06, Montreal, Quebec, H2Z 1Y6
Telephone # (514) 397-1891 – Fax (514) 397-6801

In the United States

2215 Wyoming Avenue NW, Washington, DCV 20008

Iran

The Embassy of the Islamic Republic of Iran

In Canada

245 Metcalfe Street, Ottawa, Ontario, K2P 2K2
Telephone # (613) 235-4726

Iraq

The Republic of Iraq

In Canada

215 McLeod Street, Ottawa, Ontario, K2P 0Z8
Telephone # (613) 236-9177

Flights for Umra & Hajj

Jeddah

The King Abdul Aziz International airport has three terminals; one for foreign airlines, one for Saudi Airlines and one is Madina-tul-hujjaj, which is in operation only during Hajj season.

During Umra if you fly into Jeddah by any airline other than Saudi Airlines you will disembark at the International airport. If you are intending to fly to Medina then you will have to go to another the terminal; you will have to take a taxi to take you to the Saudia terminal because all domestic flights depart from the Saudi Airlines terminal only.

You will not have to change terminals, however, if you are going straight to Makkah you will take a taxi to Makkah via Masjid al-Johfa (our Meeqat) to put on your Ihram or if it is very late then you may spend the night at a hotel in Jeddah.

During Hajj season, it does not matter which airline you fly. All Hujjaj are transferred to Madina-tu--Hujjaj and from there they either fly to Medina or if they are going to Makkah, then they will enter Makkah via Masjid al-Johfa.

During Hajj season tickets for Jeddah/Medina purchased outside Madina-tul-hujjaj are not honoured so you will have to buy your ticket from the Saudi Airlines office at Medina-tul-Hujjaj. Therefore it is highly recommended that you ask your travel agent to book for you the flight Jeddah/Medina and obtain a print out showing the PNR numbers, without this PNR # you cannot get a seat to Medina.

Normally if you fly by Saudi Airlines from New York, you arrive in Jeddah at about 4:30 PM and it takes anywhere between 6 to 8 hours to clear Immigration and customs. It is therefore, recommended that you book your flight to Medina early next morning and spend the night at Madina-tul-hujjaj.

Transportation during Umra

If you are not flying to Medina from Jeddah then you can take a white limo from the airport, which will cost you about SR500/SR600 and can accommodate four passengers and your baggage. It will take approximately four to five hours to reach Medina.

If you decide to go to Makkah from Jeddah then you can take a taxi stopping first at Masjid al-Johfa, our Meeqat, where you can do your Niyyat of Ihram and then proceed to Makkah. It will cost you about SR300/400 and can accommodate four passengers and your baggage. It will take between four to five hours to reach Makkah.

Preparation for Umra

It is very important that all Hujjaj prepare themselves mentally, physically and spiritually, months before their departure from North America. They should bear in mind that they are going to visit the Holy Cities and are **NOT** going for a holiday to visit a tourist attraction.

Information for Umra Visa

The head of each family proceeding for Umra is requested to write and enclose a self-addressed stamped envelope to the Embassy of the Kingdom of Saudi Arabia, nearest to their city of residence and request them to send enough Visa Application forms for his family. From time to time the Saudi Government amends the rules, so please refer to the enclosed instructions with the application form.

When applying for the Umra Visa you will be required to send the Saudi Embassy the following documents:

- Passport valid for a minimum six months

- A duly completed Visa application form

- A vaccination certificate against Meningitis

- A vaccination certificate against Cholera

- A copy of your marriage certificate if husband and wife are travelling to-gether

- A Mahrum certificate completed and signed by an Islamic Center

- A confirmed round trip air ticket

Please note: All Hujjaj are advised to carry with them a photocopy of their passport which shows their personal information.

American Hujjaj with green card should make sure to carry their green cards in their wallet and a copy of this card should be kept separately in a safe place.

Health Guide

- You should get a complete medical and dental check upto two months prior to your departure.

- You must start walking between 3 to 5 miles daily two months before your departure.

- Pre-travel inoculation is an effective way of reducing or eliminating the risk of several serious infections. Our doctors have recommended that all Hujjaj must take the following vaccinations which are available at all travel clinics in North America or see your family doctor.

Vaccination

- Maningococcal (Spinal Meningitis) - Compulsory

- Cholera - Compulsory

- Diphtheria-Tetanus-Polio (DTP) - Optional

- Yellow Fever - Optional

- Hepatitis A - Optional

When applying for the Umra Visa you will have to enclose certificate of vaccination against **Meningitis and Cholera** with your application form otherwise you will be denied Umra Visa.

For Ladies Only

Women should contact their family doctor well in advance to prescribe the necessary medication to avoid menstruation during the trip. Ladies in menses **cannot** enter any Masjid or any Haram of

Masoomeen A.S., but they can recite Ziyarat from outside.

Other Useful Information

Insurance

Hujjaj are recommended to take out **Medical and Accidental Insurance** coverage by Blue Cross or similar kind in other Provinces and USA for the entire trip as per their own personal needs.

Travelers Cheques

Hujjaj are advised to carry **American Express Traveler cheques** in US Dollars; they are accepted in stores in Saudi Arabia.

Currencies

Hujjaj are recommended to carry a minimum of US $500 in large bills (US $100 bill, which will fetch a better, rate than smaller bills and is easy to cash). **The bills should not be dated prior to 1990.** Please take more if you intend to do some shopping. Utmost care should be taken in hotels, whilst travelling and particularly in the Haram.

One person in a family should not keep all the money. It is advisable to make special zipped pockets on the inside of garments for safe keeping of money and valuables.

All five star hotels in Medina and Makkah offer safe deposit boxes and are available to you at no charge unless you lose your key, then it will cost you US $1000.

Credit Cards

All major credit cards are accepted in most of the stores.

Video Filming

Video filming and photographing in Saudi Arabia is prohibited, especially near the Holy Harams both in Medina and Makkah. It is better not to take with you Video or camera equipment with you.

Weather

In Saudi Arabia the temperature will vary between 20 to 248 degrees Celsius during December and January. It is particularly hot during Dhohar time. Nights in Medina are a little cooler.

Electric Current

The electric current is 220 Volts so please make sure you carry a travel adapter if you are planning to take any electrical equipment (kettle, iron, electric razor) with you an electric kettle to use on the trip.

Baggage

You must try to travel as light as possible. All baggage must be tagged with your name, full address both inside and outside and should also be locked for security purposes. The size of the suitcase should be limited to 28 inches maximum.

Laundry Facility

All hotels offer laundry facilities, which are reasonably priced. There are also many dry cleaning stores at every corner of the city and much cheaper than the hotels.

ID Card

Each person must carry an ID card showing his/her name, photograph, passport number and nationality plus some medical information and telephone numbers of the hotels they will be staying.

Respect of Holy Places

Respect and dignity of the holy places should be maintained especially while performing various rites of Ziyarat. Care should be taken to see that other Hujjaj are not inconvenienced. You are also advised not to occupy a certain place for a long time where others would like to pray. Calmness should be maintained in the **Holy Haram** and worldly talks and arguments should be avoided. While in Haram, Holy Quran, Salawat, Tasbih,Dhikar, Duas and Istighfar should be recited as much as possible.

Religious Books

Hujjaj wishing to carry duas and A'amaal books i.e. **Mafatihul-Jinan and Tohfatul Zaireen etc.** may do so by making photo copies to avoid to take the originals. Those who cannot read Arabic, you will find many Ziyarat in English in this booklet, which have been compiled with the assistance of other compilers.

Hijab

Women must wear Hijab at all times and avoid make-up during the Umra trip especially in Medina and Makkah.

A'adab

It is recommended for one to perform Ghusl (Mustahab) and be in Wudhu all the time when going to the Holy Haram.

Meeqat

Any person (not present in Makkah) who wishes to come from far to perform Umra, will have to put on the Ihram from any one of the following Meeqat (places appointed by Sharia). There are about six Meeqat if you are coming from outside of Saudi Arabia, but we will discuss only two as these are the only two that concern the pilgrims coming from North America.

• Masjid al-Shajara: This is the Meeqat, used by pilgrims who first go to Medina. It is about 7 klm from city of Medina on the way to Makkah.

• Masjid al-Johfa: Pilgrims who are going straight to Makkah from Jeddah use this Meeqat. It is about 115 Km from Jeddah on the way to Medina.

MEEQAATS

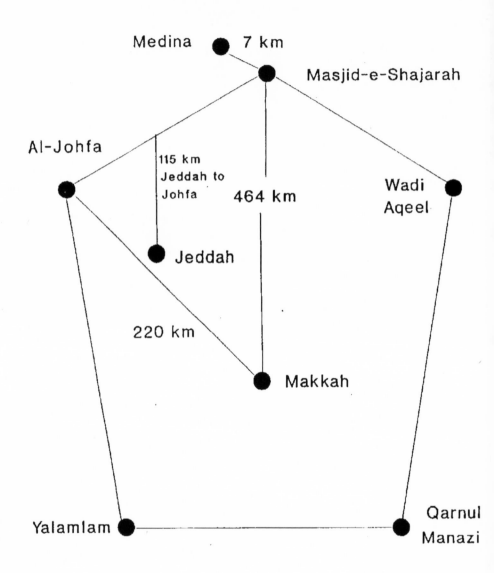

Medina ● 7 km

Masjid-e-Shajarah

Al-Johfa

115 km
Jeddah to
Johfa

464 km

Wadi
Aqeel

Jeddah

220 km

Makkah

Yalamlam

Qarnul
Manazi

Image:

MEEQAATS

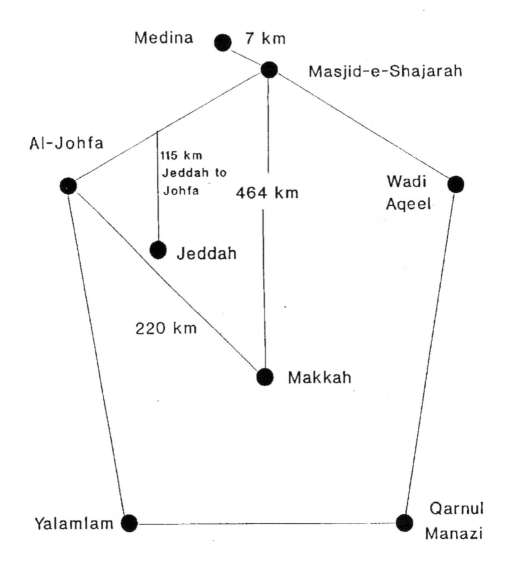

Items to take with on Your Umra Trip

Some Hujjaj have the tendency to take many unnecessary items with them. We, therefore, have prepared a list of items to be taken. Some of these items can be shared between couples and friends.

List of Items

01) One bottle of unscented Shampoo and soap.
02) One can (unscented) of dusting powder.
03) One tooth brush and toothpaste.
04) One hair brush or comb.
05) One travelling money pouch for safekeeping.
06) Four shirts, two pants, two pajamas and some undergarments for men.
07) Four sets of Shalwaar Kurta or long dress and some undergarments for women.
08) One Janamaaz (Mussalla) made of straw available in Medina. You are not allowed to use openly Sajdagha (Mor) when saying your Salaat
09) One travelling alarm clock.
10) One pair of rubber slippers and one pair of **very comfortable shoes for the daily wear.**
11) You should take enough prescription medicine to last you during the entire trip and you should carry them in your hand luggage. It is also advisable to carry a prescription of all your medication in case you have to buy them. Also please make sure to take some **Tylenol** and cough drops like **'Bradasol' for sore throat.**
12) If you wear prescription glasses then it is highly recommended to carry an extra pair with you.

New York/Jeddah

During Umra season, it is advisable to fly by Saudi Airlines from New York which flies non-stop to Jeddah and arrives at about 4:30 PM. This will give you enough time to clear immigration and customs and catch your flight to Medina which departs from Jeddah at about 8:30 PM.

Once you arrive in Medina and have collected your baggage, you will go outside the terminal and take a taxi to your hotel, which will cost you approximately SR40.

Medina

If you are staying near the Holy Haram then every morning at about 4:30 AM you should go to the Holy Haram for Salaat al-Shab also called Salaat al-Lail. Two Adhaan are given in the morning and one Ehkaam for the Fajr Salaat.

If you wish to pray inside the Haram then you should carry (with you) the straw mat because you will be able to do your prostration on it.

Also there are many small places in the Haram where there are no carpets so you can pray at these places.

After morning Salaat men proceed to Janat-ul-Baquee. The ladies will stay outside Masjid al-Nabawee waiting for the Masjid to be opened for them for Ziyarat, which is normally at about 7:00 AM.

You should try and return to your Hotel for breakfast and rest during the day and if you wish to go for Salaat at the Masjid during Dhohar and Asr, you may do so.

The Holy Haram is closed after Isha Salaat.

Salaat

Hujjaj who are required to pray **'kasar'** under normal circumstances, are recommended to pray full Salaat in Makkah and Medina, if you are staying in a Hotel near the Holy Haram.

It is highly recommended that when entering **any Masjid** for the first time then 2 rakaat Salaat be offered with the **"Niyyat of Tahiyyat al-Masjid"**

Masjid al-Nabawee

Prophet Muhammad (SAW) was born in Makkah on 17th Rabi-ul-Awwal. He was born an orphan and when he was five years old, his mother Amina Binte Wahab died. His grandfather Abdul-Muttalib who also passed away when the Prophet was only eight years old and then his uncle Abu Talib, became his guardian then brought him up.

At the age of 25 he married Bibi Khadija who was a widow of forty years of age.

When he was 40 years old, revelation came to him from Allah (SWT) ordering him to 'read in the name of Allah' and the first to know about this was Bibi Khadija and his cousin Imam Ali A.S.

During his last pilgrimage to Makkah, the Holy Prophet of Islam proclaimed at Ghadeer al-Khum that Imam Ali A.S., would be his successor, in accordance with the wishes of the Almighty Allah.

The Prophet of Islam passed away on the 28th Safar in 11 AH and is buried in the Masjid al-Nabawee.

If you follow the sketch of the Masjid al-Nabawee as shown on Page 27 you will notice that there are many pillars and places of importance, which will be explained briefly.

Bab al-Jibra'el

This is the door through which Jibra'el used to come to the chamber of Janabe Fatimah Zehra A.S.

Maqam al-Jibra'el

Whenever Jibra'el came to the Prophet of Islam with a Wahee 'revelation', he came through this door.

Stage of Suffa

The poor new Muslims who use to come to Medina from different parts of the world use to stay at this stage till they found their own shelter.

Riyadhul Jannah

The Prophet of Islam was heard saying that a piece of Jannat is between his mimber and his Zaree. Some historians say that Bibi Fatima A.S. is also buried here.

It is also said that the Prophet of Islam was heard saying that this piece of land would be raised to meet Jannat on the day of Quiyamat.

Mimber al-Rasul

This is the same mimber that the Holy Prophet (SAW) used to give khutbas from.

Mehrab al-Nabawee

Just before the mimber is the Mehrab al-Nabawee. It is from this Mehrab that the Prophet of Islam used to conduct Salaat al-Jamaat.

Pillars in Masjid al-Nabawee

Pillar of Hannaana

Adjoining the Mehrab al-Nabawee is the pillar of Hannaana. The Prophet of Allah used to lean against a date palm tree and give Khutba. After the Mimber was built, however, the Prophet (SAW) used the mimber for giving khutba. The date palm tree complained and cried because of loneliness. The Prophet of Islam reassured the date palm tree that it would accompany the Prophet in Jannat.

A pillar was erected where the pillar of Hannaanaa was.

Pillar of Aisha

It is narrated that the Prophet (SAW) was heard saying that there was one place in this Masjid where to say Salaat was great thawab but he did not say where the place was. After his death, Aisha pointed out this place where the 'Pillar of Aisha" now stands.

Pillar of Tawba

The pillar that is right in front of Kabre Mubarak is the Pillar of Tawba. It is narrated that Abu Labbaaba spied on the Prophet of Islam and went and told the Jews that there was a plan to kill them.

Abu Labbaba then repented for this mistake and he came to Masjid al-Nabawee and tied himself to a date tree, crying desperately for forgiveness.

One day when the Prophet of Allah was resting in the hujra of Umme Salma, Jibra'el came with the ayah of Quran which mentions the forgiveness of Abu Labbaaba. The Prophet untied him and gave him the good news that Allah had forgiven him. Here the Pillar was erected, it is recommended that one should try to pray two rakaats Salaat and ask for forgiveness at this pillar.

Pillar of Mahras

This pillar stands where Imam Ali A.S. used to stand guard over the Prophet of Allah when he slept at night.

Pillar of Wufood

Whenever people from outside Medina came to visit the Prophet (SAW), he would receive their delegation here.

House of Imam Hassan A.S.

When you come out through Bab al-Jibra'el and look straight towards the Qibla, you will see a white dome (silver) but now it is turned into a library and known as 'Maktab al-Sheikh-Arif Hikmat'

House of Abu Ayyub Ansari

This is the famous hadith that when the Prophet of Allah first arrived in Medina, several Ansars wanted to be his host. It was difficult for the Prophet (SAW) to decide which Ansar to choose so he announced that he would stay wherever his camel stopped.

The camel stopped in front of the House of Abu Ayyub Ansari. This is the first house in Medina where the Prophet (SAW) stayed. The house has been demolished and (now stands) in it's place the 'Court of Justice'.

Jannatul Baquee

This is the general cemetery in existence since the time of the Prophet of Islam. Here many Ashab, Momineen and Shohada al-Ohad have been buried. Also the graves of the following members of the Ahlul Bayt can be found there.

Janabe Fatima Zehra A.S.

According to some historians she is buried here.

Imam Hasan A.S.

He could not be buried next to the Prophet in Masjid al-Nabawee.

Imam Zainul Abideen A.S.

Imam Muhammad Baqar A.S.

Imam Jafar Sadiq A.S.

Janabe Fatima Binte Asad

Ummul Baneen

Wife of Imam Ali A.S. and mother of Hazrat Abbas A.S.

Janab al-Halimah

The wet nurse of the Prophet.

Janab al-Safiya and Janab al-Atika

Paternal aunts of the Prophet of Allah.

Janab al-Ruqayya, Umm al-Kulthum and Zaynab

They are the adopted daughters of the Prophet A.S.

Juwara, Saudah, Aisha, Hafsa, Umme Habibah, Umme Salma, Safiyyah & Zainab

The wives of the Prophet of Allah (SAW)

Hazrat Abbas

Uncle of the Prophet (SAW).

Janab al-Ibrahim

Son of the Prophet of Islam and brother of Bibi Fatima Zehra A.S.

Hazrat Ismail A.S.

Son of Imam Ja'far Sadique A.S.

Outside Ziyarat

If you have not joined any group and you are on your own, then you can hire a taxi to take you to all the outside Ziyarat and it will cost you approximately SR50/SR70 for four passengers.

Masjid al-Shams

It is narrated that the Prophet (SAW) fell asleep on the laps of Imam Ali A.S. just before Dhohar time till nearly Maghrib.

Imam Ali A.S. said his Dhohar and Asar Salaat sitting down. Near the time of Maghrib, the Prophet woke up and pointed his finger at the setting sun, which came up and the Prophet (SAW) prayed his Dhohar and Asr Salaat.

In Iraq there is another Masjid called **Masjid-Radus-Shams** which has got its name on a similar kind of story.

Masjid al-Zul Qibltayn

Our previous Qibla was Bait-ul-Muqaddas. The Jews used to taunt the Holy Prophet (SAW) that his followers did not have their own direction for Salaat.

One day when the Prophet of Allah (SWT) was leading the Salaat al-Dhohar, a revelation came to him after the second Rakaat to change his direction of Salaat, from Bait-ul-Muqaddas to the Ka'aba.

Masjid al-Quba

This was the first Masjid that the Prophet of Allah (SAW) built on his arrival from Makkah. It is narrated that the Prophet of Allah was heard saying that if you say two Rakaats Salaat in this Masjid you will get the Thawab of one Umra.

The Saba Saba Masjids

This was the place where the battlefield of Khandaq was fought and these Masjids were erected thereafter. There are 5 Masjid near each other. The name Khandaq was given because Salman al-Farsee dug a very big trench during this battle so that the army of the non-believers could not jump over the trench. This was the battle strategy used in Iran where Salaman al-Farsee's native country.

Masjid al-Fatah

This Masjid is situated on the hilltop. It is narrated that the Prophet of Islam stayed (in this tent) for three days in his tent and prayed for the success of the Muslims.

Masjid Salman al-Farsi

This Masjid is just at the bottom of Masjid al-Fatah. It is said that at this Masjid the tent of Salaman al-Farsee was erected.

Masjid al-Ali A.S.

This Masjid is on the hill opposite to Masjid al-Fatah where

Masjid al-Bidi Fatimah Zehra A.S.

This Masjid is at the bottom of Masjid al-Ali A.S. that was used by Bibi Fatimah Zehra A.S. Unfortunately this Masjid is now closed – (when we visited in December 1997).

Ohud – Hazrat Hamza A.S.

The lion of Allah, Hazrat Hamza A.S. the uncle of the Prophet of Islam is buried with many Shohada of Ohud here.

The Prophet (SAW) was heard saying that whoever does his Ziyarat and does not do the Ziyarat of his uncle Hamza has been unfaithful to the Prophet.

This is the place where the second Islamic war took place. At the beginning of this war the Muslims were winning, but a group of archers who were stationed at the entrance of the mountain to block the army of unbelievers, left their position to go and loot the belongings of the running away soldiers of the unbelievers, inspite of strict instructions not to leave their position, thus the battle was almost lost.

It is also narrated during this battle Jibra'el brought the sword **'Zulfiqar'** from heaven because Hazrat Ali A.S. had broken many swords.

During your stay in Medina, you should spend as much time as possible at Masjid al-Nabawee and Jannat-ul-Baquee.

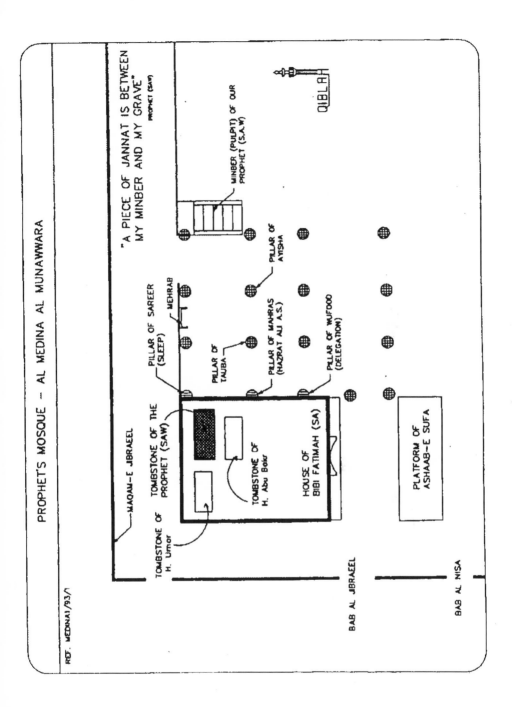

Medina/Makkah

Our experience tells us that it is advisable to depart Medina after Dhohar so (you arrive in Makkah) between Maghrib and Isha you arrive in Makkah.

If you have not joined a group and you are on your own then you will have to hire a taxi which will cost you approximately SR500/SR600 to take you to Makkah via Masjid al-Shajarah, our Meeqat, to do the Niyyat of Ihram.

You must also make sure that the limo has a permit to take Hujjaj from Medina to Makkah or else you will be turned back to Medina from the checkpoint.

You are recommended to do Sunnat Ghusl of Ihram sometime in the morning.

Niyyat: "I am doing Ghusl for the following, Sunnat Qurbatan Ilallah". You cannot use scented soap when doing this Ghusl

1. for wearing Ihram for Umra al-Mufradah

2. for entering into the Haram (Sanctified boundaries around Makkah)

3. for entering into the city of Makkah

4. for entering into the Masjid-ul-Haram

5. for doing Tawaaf of Khan al-Ka'aba

Image:

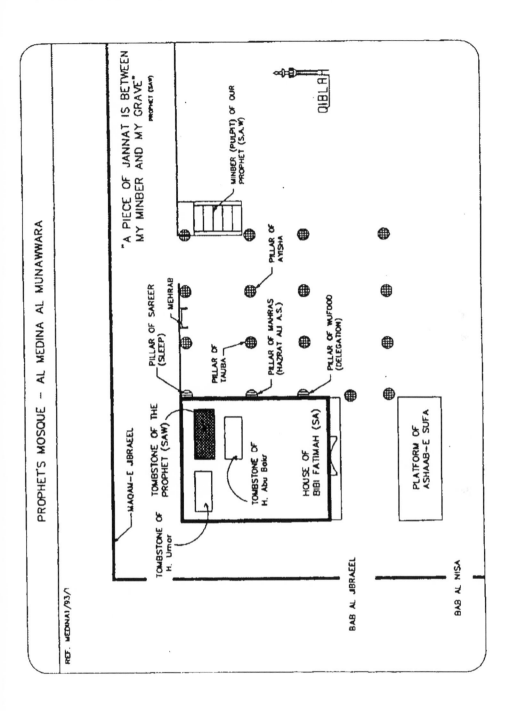

PROPHET'S MOSQUE -- AL MEDINA AL MUNAWWARA

REF. MEDINA1/93/1

"A PIECE OF JANNAT IS BETWEEN MY MINBER AND MY GRAVE" PROPHET (SAW)

QIBLAH

MINBER (PULPIT) OF OUR PROPHET (S.A.W)

PILLAR OF AYISHA

PILLAR OF SAREER (SLEEP)

MEHRAB

PILLAR OF TAUBA

PILLAR OF MAHRAS (HAZRAT ALI A.S.)

PILLAR OF WUFOOD (DELEGATION)

MAQAM-E JIBRAEEL

TOMBSTONE OF THE PROPHET (SAW)

TOMBSTONE OF H. Umar

TOMBSTONE OF H. Abu Bakr

HOUSE OF BIBI FATIMAH (SA)

PLATFORM OF ASHAAB-E SUFA

BAB AL JBRAEEL

BAB AL NISA

Umra al-Mufradah

1. To wear Ihram and Talbiya at Masjid al-Shajarah.

2. To do Tawaaf of Khane al-Ka'aba at Makkah.

3. To recite 2 Rakaat Salaat of Tawaaf at Makkah.

4. To perform Saee' at Makkah.

5. To do Taqseer at Makkah.

6. To perform Tawaaf-un-Nissa at Makkah.

7. To recite 2 Rakaat Salaat of Tawaaf at Makkah.

This Umrah is Mustahab (Sunnat). Therefore, your Niyyat while wearing the Ihram will be Mustahab, but all other A'amaals which you have to perform for completing the Umra must be done with a Wajib Niyyat.

1) Ihram And Talbiya

Ihram for men - consists of two pieces of white cloth and for **ladies** their usual daily wear is their Ihram, but it is highly recommended that it be white as it is the sign of purity.

a. For men the loins clothe covering oneself from the navel (around waist) to the knees. The second piece covers one self from the shoulders to the elbows. It is not necessary to have the clothes of Ihram on you all the time when you are in the state of Ihram. For example, one may remove the upper piece provided it is not done in front of the ladies. The Recommended size of cloth of Ihram is two and half yards in length and about 42/44 inches in breadth.

b. The cloth used for Ihram must be **Tahira.** If it becomes Najis at any time during Ihram, it must be replaced or made Tahira.

c. It must not be made of silk or golden threads.

d. It must not be Ghasbi. This means it must not be the one usurped from its rightful owner or belonging
For men the Ihram must not be sewn.

e. It must not be made of animal hide or skin.

f. Ihram can be purchased in Medina for about Saudi Riyals 30/45 per set, which is much cheaper than buying one from North America.

g. Men are allowed to wear a money belt around their waist, to secure their money, traveler's cheques and other documents. These are made of plastic and are available for about 15/30 Saudi Riyals. Ladies should either sew or buy a white pouch to wear round their neck in order to keep their money and other valuables. These are available in North America for about $8/12, depending on the quality.

h. One should try to wear your Ihram at the prescribed **Meeqat** after Dhohar prayers, or when that is not possible, after any **Wajib prayers**. But if none of the Wajib prayers precede your Niyyat for Ihram, then a minimum of two Rakaats and a maximum of 6 Rakaats (by way of 2 Rakaats in each set, like the morning Salaat) is Mustahab.

• **Niyyat: "I am wearing Ihram for Umra al-Mufradah Qurbatan Illallah".**

After wearing the Ihram immediately proclaim Talbiyya. Men must recite loudly but women **should not** recite loudly. Talbiyya must be recited in Arabic as under

"Labbaik, Allahumma Labbaik, Labbaik La
Sharika Laka Labbaik, Innal Hamda Wan
Ne'amata Laka Walmuka La Sharika Laka Labbaik"
"Here I am, O Lord, here I am, You indeed have no partner, here I am. No Doubt, all praise and bounties are Yours, and so is the absolute Domain. You indeed have no partners, here I am".

With Talbiyya recited, the process of wearing Ihram is now completed. **Twenty-five** things become **Haraam** and forbidden for you as long as you are in Ihram. They are applicable to both, men and women.
These are:

The Following 25 Things Become Haraam

1. **Hunting:** Remember that hunting within the sacred area around and in Makkah, known as the **Haram**, is always forbidden. It is not confined to Ihram. When in Ihram, hunting anywhere also is forbidden. You are allowed to kill scorpions, pythons, poisonous snakes and rats. You are allowed also to slaughter domestic fowls such as goats, sheep, camels, etc.

2. **Sexual intercourse:** Sexual intercourse, or any acts of courtship which would arouse sexual desire are forbidden. Even lustful glance at ones own wife or husband or any other lady or man who is **Na-Mahram** is forbidden. The expiation is one camel or a cow or a sheep in that order of affordability.

3. **Masturbating:** This includes all methods of self-abuse. It has the same precept as sexual intercourse.

4. **Marriage contract:** To read **Nikah** for oneself or for others regardless of whether the other person is in Ihram or not. This applies to **Muta'a** as well. The expiation is ihtiyatan (precautionary) one sheep.

5. **Perfumes:** To use perfume or apply it on ones clothes. Perfumes like **Saffron, Camphor, Cloves, Cardamom, Amber and** all their uses are forbidden. Sweet smelling fruits like apples etc., may be eaten, but it is forbidden to smell them.

6. **Smell or odor:** To close ones nose or nostrils from bad smell or **odor** is not allowed. The expiation of doing so is one sheep. However, there is no objection if one hastily passes away from the unpleasant odour.

7. **Sewn clothes:** It is **Haram** for men to wear sewn or stitched clothes in **Ihram.** Their clothes must not have sleeves or seams. However, belts with sewn pockets for keeping money, traveler's cheques, passports and other valuables, slung around the shoulders or worn around the waist are allowed. Similarly, **Hernia** belts can be worn. One is not allowed to fasten the Ihram with pins or a needle or anything of that sort. You can not even tie a knot. Ladies are allowed to wear all types of sewn clothes during **Ihram**, except for the hand gloves and wear a **veil.** The expiation for violation of this rule is one sheep.

8. **Surma:** To apply black surma (eyeliner) in the eyes for cosmetic purposes are strictly forbidden for men and women. If it is neither black nor for any cosmetic or beautifying purposes, then it is allowed. The expiation of violation is one sheep.

9 Mirror: To look into a mirror for cosmetic reason, which means to appreciate ones looks and features, including combing hair etc., is forbidden. The expiation of this violation is one sheep. If a driver wearing Ihram has to refer to the mirrors of his car or bus as he drives, there is no objection. Spectacle glasses are allowed provided they are not worn for fashion or beautification, though this should be avoided if possible.

10. **Lying and abusing:** To tell lies or abuse and scorn is always forbidden but when in Ihram it becomes all the more undesirable and Haraam. Similarly, it is Haraam to boast or brag about ones own superiority or excellence, with an intention to belittle or under estimate the others.

Note: This means one has to be very careful not to use abusive, foul or obscene language in ordinary conversation. If this is done the expiation is one cow for violation of this rule.

11. Shoes and socks: It is forbidden for men to cover the upper part of the feet from the toes to the ankle. So, men must not wear socks or full shoes. Women can wear them, (although), it is better for women to avoid wearing socks. The expiation for men violating of this rule is one sheep.

12. Swearing: To take an oath or to swear in any form, particularly saying LaWallah, Balaa Wallah (no, by God or yes, by God) is Haraam. The expiation is **Istegfaar,** (repentance) for the first and second time, and a sheep for the third time.

The following cases are exceptional.

a) That it is intended to prove thereby some right or to make the wrong public to others.

b) That is not meant to swear thereby, but is merely expressing respect and love.

There is no expiation (kafara) for a right swearing, provided, it is not more than twice, otherwise, the expiation is one sheep. If it is a wrong swearing, the expiation is one sheep for the first time, for the second time two sheep and a cow for the third time.

13. Killing insects: It is forbidden to kill insects or brush-off an insect originating from one's own body e.g. lice. There is no harm to transfer them from one place to another and the expiation for this rule being violated is to give a handful of food to the poor.

14. Make up: All methods of self-beautification, either by use of cosmetics or by ornaments are forbidden. A ring worn for the Niyyat of thawab, like a **Firoza or Aqeeq or Dhoor al-Najaf** is permissible. Ladies must also refrain from wearing ornaments, except those they usually wear. But even these must not be displayed to men, even to the husband.

15. Henna: To apply henna is Haraam during Ihram. The expiation for the violation is ihtiyatan (precautionary) one sheep.

16. **Pulling out of a tooth:** To have your tooth extracted even if there is no bleeding due to it. **(Marhum Ayatullah Abul Qassim El Khui did not lay emphasis on this. He said this is permitted).**

17. Blood: To take out blood from ones own body, or to cause any bleeding by scratching or brushing the teeth etc., is Haraam. However, if this becomes in evitable for relief from any distress, it is allowed. The expiation for ignoring this rule is one sheep.
Note: One should use salt to brush teeth rather than scented toothpaste.

18. Covering of the face: In the state of Ihram, women are not allowed to cover their faces with a mask or veil, not even partly. While saying her Salaat, they may cover part of their forehead etc., in an effort to cover her head and hair fully, but after Salaat, she has to see that her face is not covered even partially. She can cover her face while sleeping. She must also refrain from immersing her head in water. Men are not allowed to cover their face at all, their ears must also be visible.

Men must not carry any baggage on their heads, nor dip themselves in water. However, a handkerchief or strip of cloth tied on the forehead for relief from a headache is allowed. The expiation for this violation is one sheep.

19. Ointment: It is forbidden to apply any kind of ointment to the body, whether it has a sweet smell or not. If however, it becomes necessary for medical reasons it is allowed.

20. To remove or pluck hair from ones own body, or from another's body, regardless of whether the other fellow is in Ihram or not. The expiation for this is a handful of grain. There are four exceptions to this.

i) If hair falls itself, while doing Wudhu or Ghusl, there is no objection.

ii) If one's hair has grown to his/her eyelid and is causing distress and agony, one may remove it.

iii) If the removal of hair becomes inevitable for any good reason and valid reason. But if due to the hair, there are too many lice on the body, and it becomes necessary to remove the hair so as to be relieved of the parasite.

iv) You are allowed to stroke your hair or beard or slowly scratch your body, if you know that by so doing no hair would fall, and no bleeding would be caused.

20. **Travel:** Men are not permitted to travel under any kind of shade or shadow, be it the hood of a car, an umbrella or walking in the shadow of a car, bus, caravan or aircraft. All travelling must be under the open sky. Shades are permitted at the time of resting or taking a respite on the way. You can ward off sunrays by cupping one hand. The meaning of refraining from shade or shadow is that men must not protect themselves from sunrays, cold, heat or rain. So it is not only the head, which must not go into shade, it is the whole body. Once you are in Makkah, you are allowed to go under shade or shadow, even before you have found your accommodation or place of abode. Women, children and such men who fear that exposure would disable them or render them very sick, are exempted. But for such men, the expiation (Kafara) will have to be given inspite of the valid excuse they may have. The expiation for this violation is one sheep.

According to Ayatullah Sayyid Seestani, he allows men to travel in closed bus during the night. Men may follow his rulings if they are doing his Taqleed.

21. **Cutting of nails:** Cutting of nails either whole or partly is not allowed unless the nail is causing pain. The expiation (Kafara) for each fingernail being cut is a handful of food. If all nails of the hands are cut in the same place, the expiation (Kafara) will be one sheep. The same is true of feet. If the nails of both the hands and feet are cut in the same place, the expiation will be one sheep. If one cuts the nails of his hand in one place and the feet in another place the expiation will be two sheep.

23. Carrying of weapons: One is not allowed to carry any weapons, unless it is absolutely necessary. There is no harm in carrying a knife, etc., for cutting fruits, etc.

24. Uprooting trees: To uproot, pluck or cut the grass, leaves of the trees and all that grows from the earth in Makkah and around it; is not allowed. This is forbidden during Ihram and also without Ihram.

25. Nikah: To be witness to somebody's Nikah.

Note: All the expiation can be paid in Makkah or after returning home or even by sending money to a third world country for the same purpose with the exception of hunting which must be paid in Makkah.

The above rules are according to Marhum Ayoutallah Abul Qassim Al Khoei. If you are a Muqaleed of another Ayatullah please make sure you check his rulings with an A'alem.

Makkah

Upon arrival in Makkah you will check into your hotel where you are booked to stay (and after refreshing yourself and having your dinner) you will then Inshallah proceed to the Holy Haram to perform all the A'amaal of Umrah al-Mufradah.

Conditions Before Tawaaf

Wudhu is Wajib for Tawaaf, as is Ghusl, if necessary due to its known causes, (Janabat, Haiz or Nifas). One must be free of all these states before Tawaaf.

If for any justifiable excuse, Ghusl or Wudhu cannot be performed, then you have to do **Tayammum** instead before performing Tawaaf. Women in Istehaddha would follow the rules, as in Salaat, that is, they would do Tawaaf after performing Ghusl and Wudhu. When Wudhu becomes Batil during Tawaaf, (or when a woman finds that her menses etc., have commenced, there are rules to follow.

a. If Wudhu is Batil before or just at half of the total Tawaaf, that is three and half rounds, Tawaaf is Batil. Do your Wudhu again and repeat the Tawaaf.

b. If Wudhu is Batil unintentionally at the completion of the **fourth** round, you have to do Wudhu and continue further. There is no need to repeat the whole Tawaaf.

c. If one makes his/her Wudhu Batil intentionally at any state, he/she will do Wudhu and repeat the Tawaaf, making **Niyyat** that he/she is completing the circuits, which are due.

For ladies only: When a lady experiences menses while performing Tawaaf, she must come out of Masjid-ul-Haraam immediately. If she has then completed half of the Tawaaf, which is three and half rounds, those are valid. When she becomes **Tahira**, after her Ghusl, she will complete the balance. Agha Khui had said that it is Ahwat (recommended) that she make a new Tawaaf of seven rounds with a Niyyat to relieve her of whatever is incumbent upon her.

If a woman completes Tawaaf and she sees blood before she can say her Salaat al-Tawaaf, she will come out of the Masjid-ul-Haraam immediately. Her Tawaaf will remain valid, and she will wait until she is Tahira, and after Ghusl, she will say her Salaat al-Tawaaf. In case there is no time and she must go to Arafah, Muzdhalifah etc., then will do Saee' and Taqseer, complete her Hajj A'amaal upto Munna, and before the Tawaaf of Hajj al-Tamattu', she must first pray the Salaat of Tawaaf which she had left.

If a woman is not sure whether her menses began after the Tawaaf and its' Salaat or during or before, her Tawaaf and Salaat, will be deemed correct.

A woman who is not able to perform Tawaaf and its' Salaat because of Haiz or Nifas, and is also unable to do Ghusl, will do **Tayammum** instead of Ghusl and perform the Tawaaf and its' Salaat.

It is Ahwat (recommended) that she appoint a Naib who would do these A'amaal on her behalf.

The body and clothes must be Tahira. Even small stains or dots of blood that are permissible in daily prayers are not allowed in Tawaaf.

However, if you have a boil or a wound, which persistently bleeds, and it cannot be removed from the body or the dress, then it is permissible.

Private parts must be adequately covered during Tawaaf, the same as is done in Salaat. The clothes of Ihram must not be Ghasbi (as already explained under Ihram).

For men only: Men must have been **circumcised** before Tawaaf can be valid. This includes sensible boys as well. It is Ahwat (recommended) that younger boys, who are not even able to wear Ihram by themselves be also circumcised.

Mustahab (Sunnat) Acts of Tawaaf

1. To recite Dhikar Quran, Salawaat or Dua during Tawaaf.
2. To be barefoot.
3. To take short steps, walking with total calm and composure, portraying full reverence.
4. To avoid useless talks and movements.
5. To close your eyes during Tawaaf (if possible).
6. To do Tawaaf at dhohar time (mid-day hours if possible).
7. To remain nearer to Ka'aba.
8. To salute **Hajarul Aswad** in every round, by raising your palms towards it and reciting **"Bismillahi, Allahu Akbar"** and after your Tawaaf is complete to try and kiss Hajarul Aswad without causing inconvenience to other people by way of pushing etc.
9. At the **Mustajar,** the back wall of Ka'aba near Rukne Yamani, it is Mustahab to stand there on the seventh round and raise your hands in dua and supplication, to touch the wall with your cheek and body, in all humility and with confessions of sins, seeking forgiveness. It is also a place to pray Haajat.

There will be thousands of people doing Tawaaf and the best place to enter into the crowd is from somewhere near Hajre Ismail and slowly working your way into the crowd.

The first cycle will commence from Hajarul Aswad. Try to be as close as possible near the walls of the Ka'aba. When you reach Rukne Yamani, you should start making your Niyyat.

2) Tawaaf of Khana al-Ka'aba

Niyyat: "I am going round this Ka'aba seven times for Umra al-Mufradah Qurbatan Ilallah."

How to do Tawaaf

1. The starting and ending point of each circuit during Tawaaf is Hajarul-Aswad.

After making your Niyyat, stand just parallel to Hajarul Aswad and start the Tawaaf. Each round is completed when you return to the starting point.

2. At all the time during Tawaaf, the Ka'aba must remain to your left. Your left shoulder should **not** turn away from the Ka'aba, otherwise that particular sector of movement will not be included in Tawaaf. You will have to return to the place where you were distracted and continue from there. The Ka'aba is in a cubical shape, it has four corners. As you come to a corner of the Ka'aba, you will make a gradual turn exercising care, as much as possible, that your shoulder remains parallel to Ka'aba.

3. There is a small arc shaped wall shape adjoining Ka'aba on one side. This is **Hijre Ismail**. (The graves of Hazrat Ismail, his mother Hajira and other Prophets). While making Tawaaf, this Arc must be included in the round. If you pass between the Ka'aba and Hijre Ismail during Tawaaf, that particular circuit will be void. So, you will have to repeat the circuit. It is Ahwat, (recommended) to not touch Hijre Ismail. It is Ahwat (recommended) not placing your hands on Hijre Ismail during Tawaaf.

4. The area of Tawaaf is defined as one between Ka'aba and Maqam al-Ibrahim. This is about 40 feet or 26 and half arm lengths. Tawaaf must be carried out within this area, and not beyond. As mentioned earlier, Hijre Ismail is adjoining Ka'aba. It covers nearly 31 feet of space left. So, when you reach here, you find only 9 feet of open space on the left. You will keep yourself within this area during Tawaaf. Agha Khui had said that Tawaaf beyond its area would not be correct. But if it becomes extremely difficult to do so due to the great number of people, or other disabilities, then Tawaaf beyond the described area would be deemed sufficient.

5. Around the Ka'aba near its foundation, there are small supporting walls. During Tawaaf, one must not pass over them. If one passes over them, or touches them during Tawaaf, it will be necessary to repeat the part of the circuit which was done on the said walls, and then, it would be Ahwat to repeat the whole Tawaaf all over.

6. The number of circuits in each Tawaaf is **Seven.** Each round begins from Hajarul Aswad and ends there. A Tawaaf of less or more then seven rounds is Batil.

Simple rule to remember when you are in doubt about the number of circuits or rounds:

The following doubts should be ignored:

• All doubts after the completion of Tawaaf or after having moved from the place of Tawaaf, should be ignored.

• When you are certain of having completed the seven rounds, but are doubtful whether you went round more than seven times, such doubts should also be ignored.

• If you were doing Tawaaf that is Wajib, all doubts during Tawaaf would render Batil. When in doubt whether the round is third or fourth, for example you will decide that it is third, complete the Tawaaf, and do it all over again. So the rule is that, determine the lesser number, complete the doubtful Tawaaf, and then repeat the whole set again.

• If your Tawaaf is Mustahab, determine the lesser number and complete your Tawaaf. It would be correct.

• You can rely on your friend or companion who is doing Tawaaf with you. For example, if he/she tells you that the particular round is fifth, and if he/she says so with certitude, you can accept it.

• **Muwalaat** is necessary in Tawaaf. This means that all seven rounds must follow each other in sequence. However, if one wishes to take a brief respite or rest during Tawaaf, one may do so provided that it is not too long to disrupt Muwalaat.

3) Salaat of Tawaaf

Niyyat: "I am offering two Rakaat Salaat for Tawaaf of Umra al-Mufradah Qurbatan Ilallah".

Salaat of Tawaaf: Two rakaats of Salaat of Tawaaf becomes Wajib immediately after completion of Tawaaf.

This Salaat must be said behind Maqame-Ibrahim, or at a place nearest to it. The method of this Salaat is exactly like the morning Salaat. But in this, you may recite the suras loudly or silently, as you prefer.

4) Saee'

The Niyyat should be made at the hill of Safaa. Your walk will start from Safaa and end at Marwa.

Niyyat: "I walk between Safaa and Marwah, seven times for Umra al-Mufradah Qurbatan Ilallah".

Saee" means to walk between the two mountains **Safaa** and **Marwaa.** It begins from Safaa and ends at Marwaa.

Each Saee' consists of seven trips. As you walk from Safaa ending at Marwaa, this is counted as first, your return from Marwaa to Safaa will be second and so on and you will end your seventh round at Marwaa.

Mustahab acts of Saee'

a. Although Wudhu or even Ghusl is not a pre-requisite for Saee' it is Mustahab to be in a purified state.

b. To do Saee' with a minimum of delay after Salaat al-Tawaaf.

c. To Kiss or Salute Hajarul Aswad before when you are proceeding for Saee', (of course if this is possible).

d. To drink from Zam Zam before going for Saee'. It is also Mustahab to pour the water upon ones head and body

e. To go to Safaa through **Babus Safaa**, the door facing Hajarul Aswad.

f. To proceed with humility, reverence and composed frame of mind.

g. To climb the steps of Safaa.

h. To kiss the corner of the Stone in Safaa.

i. To utter words of praise and gratitude for Allah, remembering His bounties, blessings, signs and kindness.

j. To stand longer at Safaa.

k. To conduct the Saee' calmly and with reverence.

l. It is Mustahab for men to do Harwala (jogging or trotting) between the two green lights. For ladies, it is Mustahab to quicken the pace.

Points to remember:

a. Saee' is Wajib, and must be performed immediately after Salaat of Tawaaf.

b. Wudhu or Ghusl is not necessary for Saee' though it is better to be with.

c. While walking from Safaa to Marwaa, and similarly from Marwaa to Safaa, you must walk forward facing the rocks. If you walk in reverse, then the distance covered this way will have to be retraced. There is no harm if you look sideways or behind during the walk.

d. To rest at Safaa or Marwaa is allowed during Saee', it is Ahwat not to rest between the rocks.

e. Saee' can be performed walking or on the back of an animal, or on somebody's shoulders, or on a wheelchair or cart etc. When all these alternatives are not possible you have to appoint someone as Naib, who will do the Saee' on your behalf.

f. The distance between Safaa and Marwaa must be crossed on the route that is fixed. Your walking may not strictly be in a straight line but you cannot deviate from the given route.

g. In between Safaa and Marwaa, there are two pillars, which are meant for Harwala. In these days, they are built of green stones, distinguishing them from the others. When one reaches these, one has to trot or jog. This is Mustahab for men only.

h. When one is in doubt the number of trips one has made, Saee' would be Batil. The rule to be followed is exactly like that of doubts during Tawaaf.

5) Taqseer

Niyyat: "I am performing Taqseer so as to be relieved of Ihram for Umra al-Mufradah Qurbatan Ilallah".

Taqseer means cutting off some hair or nails. Taqseer had to be done after completion of your Saee' at Marwa (it can be done at your hotel).

PS In Ihram one cannot cut his or another person's hair until and unless one has got his/her Taqseer done first by a person who is already out of the Ihram.

6) Tawaaf-un-Nissa

Niyyat: "I am doing Tawaaf-un-Nissa by going round this Ka'aba seven times for Umra al-Mufradah Qurbatan Ilallah".

7) Salaat of Tawaaf-un-Nisa

Niyyat: "I am offering two Rakaat Salaat for Tawaaf-un-Nissa for Umra al-Mufradah Qurbatan Ilallah".

Points to Remember Regarding Tawaaf-un-Nissa

This Tawaaf is Wajib for each and every person, whether you are a man, a woman, or a child. If it were omitted, sexual relations between married partners would be Haraam. Those who are doing Niyyabat must remember that while doing this Tawaaf, their Niyyat, would not be for themselves, but for the person, whom they are representing as a Naib.

If somebody avoids Tawaaf-un-Nissa purposely, or because of not knowing the law, he/she has too later perform it himself/herself, and as long as he/she has not done it, his wife/husband would remain Haraam to him/her. Naib for this Tawaaf is only allowed if it was omitted forgetfully, or for ladies who due to their menses etc., are unable to do it. This Tawaaf is Wajib for children as well, if they have worn Ihram.

During your entire stay in Makkah you should try and visit the Holy Haram as much as possible to Sunnat Tawaaf as many as you can for your deceased parents, relatives and friends. You do not need to be in Ihram. But if you wish to do Umra for your passed away parents, relatives or friends then you must to go to Masjid al-Umra just outside of Makkah, do your Niyyat, go to Masjid-u--Haraam and do the Umrah, (exactly the same A'amals that you did when you arrived from Medina).

Ziyarats in & Around Makkah

Ka'aba

Which stands majestically in the center of Masjid-ul-Haraam. The Ka'aba was first built by Prophet Adam exactly under Baitul Mamoor which is in Jannat.

It is said that after the strong waves and currents of Prophet Nuh's A.S. ship, the Ka'aba was destroyed except for the foundation. Prophet Ibrahim later built the walls of the Ka'aba again. During the time of the Prophet of Allah, the people were still idol worshippers.

Our fist Imam, Hazrat Ali A.S. was born in the Ka'aba and one can still notice the crack in the wall which opened up to allow Bibi Fatima Binte Asad A.S. to enter few days before the birth or our Imam.

Hajr al-Ismail

In this arc Hazrat Ismail, Bibi Hajra and many prophets are buried. It is great thawab to recite two rakaat Salaat. If you are standing in the arc and if you raise your head to see the top of the Ka'aba you will see a golden pipe was draining out rain water on the Ka'aba. This is the place where you should ask for your Haajat. Here are the graves of Bibi Hajra and his son Hazrat Ismail. It is also believed that other Prophets are also buried here.

Hajr-ul-Aswad

This is the black stone from Heaven. It is narrated that Prophet Adam A.S. (when he was in Heaven), he used to sit on this stone and pray.

When Prophet Adam A.S. was sent down to the earth as a calipha, the stone started crying because it was missing the company of Hazrat Adam, so Allah (SWT) sent this stone to the earth and the angels put it in the Ka'aba. On the day of judgement it is a witness for those who have gone for Hajj and Umrah.

Makaam al-Ibrahim

There is a footprint of Prophet Ibrahim (which can be seen through the glass) when he used to put his foot on it when building the walls of the Ka'aba.

Zam Zam

By the order of Allah (SWT), Prophet Ibrahim left is wife Hajra and his son Ismail on the plains close to where the Ka'aba is situated to spread the word of God. Hazrat Ismail became thirsty so Bibi Hajra went to look for water. She went running seven times between the Hills of Safa and Marwa but could not find water.

While Bibi Hajra desperately searching for water, Hazrat Ismail rubbed his feet on the ground as he was very thirsty and through the miracle of Allah (SWT) water sprang furiously near the feet of Hazrat Ismail, so much water sprang forth that Bibi Hajra shouted 'Zam Zam' which means 'stop'. The well of Zam Zam is still there but now instead a well you see some pipes which brings the water supply to the Masjid and to the whole of Makkah. It is said that the water level is the same, and it is pure and free from any kind of dirt or germs.

Hills of Safa and Marwa

These are the same two hills between which Bibi Hajra ran between them seven times to look for water for Hazrat Ismail. Allah (SWT) loved this act of hers so much that He made it obligatory on Hajjis who are performing Hajj and Umra.

Janatul-Mualla

This is a general cemetery in existence since the time of the Prophet and many Ulemas, relatives of the Prophet (SAW) and many well known personalities are buried here including:

Janab al-Khadijatul Kubra

She was very rich prosperous and successful businesswoman who entrusted the Prophet of Allah with her caravan going to Syria, Egypt and other places; she later married the Prophet (SAW) at the age of 40.

Janab al-Abu Talib

He was the father of our first Imam. He died when the Prophet of Allah was 50 years old.

Janab al-Abdul Mutalib

He was the Prophet of Islam (SAW) paternal grandfather.

Hazrat Abdullah

He was the father of our Prophet (SAW) and it is narrated that when Masjid al-Nabawee in Medina was being extended, his grave was dug and his body which was intact was transferred to Jannat-ul-Maulla.

Hazrat Amina Bint al-Wahab

She was the mother of our Prophet (SAW) who died when he was only 5 years old. Some historians say that she is buried at Jannatul-Mualla and some say she is buried at a place called Abawa.

Masjid al-Jinn

A group of Jinn were passing by, when they heard the Prophet of Allah (SAW) reciting the Holy Quran. They were so moved and came to the Prophet, repented and accepted Islam. A Masjid was later built here called Masjid al-Jinn.

Cave of Thawr

During the Hijrah the Holy Prophet (SAW) (with Abu Bakr) stayed here for three days. The Miraculous incident of a spider's web and a pigeon laying eggs occurred at the mouth of this cave. This misled the trackers and the Prophet of Allah (SAW) was safe.

Cave of Hira

The first 'revelation' of "Iqra Bismi Rabbek" was revealed here.

Arafah

It is also known as the 'tent' city that comes into existence only one day in a year and this on the 9th of Dhulhijja when all Hajjis are required to stay here from Dhohar until Maghrib.

It is said that this is the first place where Prophet Adam A.S. and Bibi Havva met for the first time after they were asked to leave Jannat.

Jabal al-Rahmah

This mountain is in Arafah. During Umra season one can climb it by steps and it is highly recommended to pray two rakaat Salaat of Haajat and then ask for your Hakata.

Muzdhalifa or Ma'shar

The Hajjis are required to spend the night here and also collect 70 pebbles for hitting the Shaitaan in Munna.

Munna

This is a city that comes to existence for three days in a whole year. All the Hajjis are required to spend the night in Munna, to hit the three Shaitaans and sacrifice of an animal. Men must also to do Taqseer or Halaq. Women are required to do Taqseer and not Halaq.

Masjid al-Kheef - In Munna

It is highly recommended to pray 6 rakaat Salaat in this Masjid that has great thawab as it is said that many Prophets of Allah prayed here.

Hajj al-Tul Islam

Hajj al-tul Islam or Wajib Hajj is obligatory once in a lifetime upon all Muslims and the following conditions must be obtained before Hajj becomes Wajib.

1. Baligh, means age of puberty, girls 9 years of age and boys 15 years of age.

2. A'Aaqil, means being sane and of sound mind.

3. Istita'ah. Means capability. This means one must be able to defray all the necessary expenses during Hajj, including the return passage.

• If he has dependents, he must be able to maintain himself and his family.

• Upon his return, he must have enough means to maintain himself and his family.

• The journey to Hajj and returning from it must not involve any danger to the security of his life, wealth and family.

• One intending to go to Hajj must be healthy. If he is infirm or old or has any other justifiable excuse Hajj would not be Wajib, though if other conditions were fulfilled, however, he must send someone as his **Naib (agent representative).**

• Ample time must be there for one to prepare to go to Hajj, and to perform all the obligatory acts. If other conditions of Hajj are met, while time is limited or extraordinary effort is involved, one has to keep the money unused until the following year for the purpose.

When above conditions are fulfilled, Hajj, becomes Wajib immediately. To postpone it without any reasonable excuse is among the major s**ins**. Hajj, must be performed in the same year of Istita'ah, and it continues to remain obligatory in the ensuing years as long as it has not been performed.

Important

Before leaving for Hajj, make sure that:
a) You fully understand the rules of **Taqleed.**

b) Your money is clean, and you have paid your obligatory debts like **Khums** and **Zakat.** These essential, long term debts like house mortgages, business loans, car loans, furniture loans, etc., are not considered as debts for **Hajj** purposes, provided the installments are met by you without any hardship.

c) Your intention is purely for **Hajj**. The **Niyyat** must be to perform Hajj for the sake of seeking nearness to Allah, Qurbatan Illallahi.

d) You have prepared your **Will,** and given some "**sadaqa"** for your safe journey.

Requirement When Applying For Hajj Visa

When applying for the Umra Visa you will be required to send the Saudi Embassy the following documents:
• Passport valid for a minimum six months

• A duly completed Visa application

• A vaccination certificate against Meningitis

• A vaccination certificate against Cholera

• A copy of your marriage certificate if husband and wife are travelling to-gether

• Each woman travelling must have a Mahrum certificate completed and signed by an Islamic Centre

• A confirmed round trip air ticket

• Two drafts **one for SR444** payable to the UNIFIED AGENTS OFFICE IN JEDDAH and the **second for SR435** payable to AUTOMOBILES UNION OF SAUDI ARABIA drawn on a bank in Saudi Arabia.

• Non American Citizens should submit to the Consular Section (their American Green Card) and must travel to Jeddah without making a stop to their respective countries.

• Ladies over the age of 45 going to HAJJ should submit the necessary notarized legal documents to prove the relationship of the Mahram, otherwise they can travel with an organized group and submit a no-objection letter from their husband or son. A legal notary should notarize such a letter. Moreover, the accompanying Mahram will be forbidden to leave the Kingdom on his own.

Please refer to the instructions sent by the Saudi Embassy when they send the application form to you.

Items to Take for Hajje-Tul Islam

For a couple (husband and wife)

• One bath towel each.

• One small plastic bottle of unscented shampoo each.

• One small cake of unscented bath soap (Dove) each.

• One small can of unscented dusting powder each.

• One travelling toothbrush and tooth paste each.

• One hair brush and comb each.

• One pair of rubber beach slippers (not stitched) each.

• One money belt for man (not stitched) available at Medina-tul-Hujjaj (Jeddah airport) or in Medina for approximately SR 15 to 20.

• One pouch for woman to be worn around the neck for securing money and other valuables (can be purchased from any camping or travelling store in North America) at approximately $10.

• One set of Ihram for man available at Medina-tul-Hujjaj

(Jeddah Airport) approximately SR 35 to 45.Two shirts, two pants or white cotton pajamas and some undergarments for men (preferably cotton and hand washable).
• Four sets of shalwaar kurta or long dress for women and some undergarments (preferably cotton and hand washable). **Chadhar is necessary.**

One small folding umbrella (preferably white) and a hand fan for women.
One mussalaa (janamaaz) made of straw, each available at Medina-tul-Hujjaj.
One small plastic tube of unscented Vaseline to be shared between the couple.
• One small water sprayer to spray cold water on oneself whilst travelling especially to Arafah, Muzdhalifah and Munna. It is necessary for each Hujjaj to carry this and must be taken from North America.

• One sleeping bag preferably made of cotton and weighing between 2 to 2 and half pounds.

• One bed sheet each.

• If you are wearing prescribed glasses then it is advisable to take a back up pair.

• One pair of sun glasses each (option).

• One cloth bag with shoulder strap to carry your shoes when going to the Holy Haram.

• One pair of rubber slippers and one pair of **very comfortable shoes for daily wear.**

• You should take enough prescription medicine to last you during the entire trip and you should carry with them in your hand luggage. It is also advisable to carry a prescription of all your medication in case you have to by them. Also make sure to take some **Tylenol** and cough drops like **'Bradasol'** for sore throat.

• If you wear prescription eyeglasses then it is highly recommended you carry an extra pair.

Hajje-tul-Islam

Wajib Hajj is known as Hajj-tul-Islam that has two parts. The first part is called Umra al-Tamauttu' and the second part is called Hajj al-Tamattu'.

1) Umra al-Tamattu' 2) Hajj al-Tamattu'

It is recommended to take Sunnat Ghusl before you put on your Ihram.

Niyyat: "I am doing Ghusl for the following, Qurbatan Ilallah".

1) For wearing Ihram for Umra al-Tamattu'

2) for entering into the Haram (Sanctified boundaries around Makkah)

3) for entering into the city of Makkah

4) for entering into the Masjid-ul-Haram

5) for doing Tawaaf of Khan al-Ka'aba

Caution: You are not allowed to use scented soap or scented shampoo when doing this Ghusl.

Umrah al-Tamattu'

1) To wear Ihram at Masjid al-Shajarah/Masjid al-Johfa
2) To proclaim Talbiya after wearing the Ihram
3) To do Tawaaf of Khane al-Ka'aba at Makkah
4) To recite 2 Rakaat Salaat of Tawaaf at Makkah
behind Makam al-Ebrahim
5) To perform Saee' at Makkah
6) To do Taqseer at Makkah

PS There is no Tawaaf-un-Nissa at this point. You will perform it with the A'amaal of Hajj al-Tamattu.'

1) Ihram and Talbiya

To wear Ihram at Masjid al-Shajarah if you are going to Makkah from Medina or Masjid al-Johfa if you are going to Makkah from Jeddah.

Niyyat: "I am wearing Ihram for Umra al-Tamattu' for Hajje-tul-Islam, Qurbatan Ilallah"

As soon as you have done your Niyyat of Ihram and proclaimed Talbiya, 25 things become Haram as shown on
page 33.

2) Tawaaf of Khan al-Ka'aba

Niyyat: "I go round this Ka'aba seven times for Umra al-Tamattu' for Hajje-tul-Islam, Qurbatan Ilallah"

3) Salaat of Tawaaf

This Salaat is to be performed as near as possible behind Makam al-Ibrahim but facing the Ka'aba.

Niyyat: "I am offering two Rakaat Salaat for Tawaaf of Umra al-Tamattu' for Hajje-tul-Islam Qurbatan Ilallah".

4) Saee'

Niyyat: "I walk between Safaa and Marwah, seven times for Umra al-Tamattu', for Hajje-tul-Islam, Qurbatan Ilallah".
The Niyyat should be made on the hill of Safaa.

5) Taqseer

Niyyat: "I am performing Taqseer so as to be relieved of Ihram for Umra al-Tamattu', for Hajje-tu--Islam, Qurbatan Ilallah".

Taqseer means cutting off some hair or nails and has to be done after completion of your Saee' at Marwa or can be done at your place of residence.

PS: In Ihram one cannot cut his or another person's hair unless and until one has got his/her Taqseer done first by a person who is already out of Ihram.

You must have noticed that there is no **Tawaaf-un-Nisa** at this point, you will perform it after you complete all A'amaal of Hajj al-Tamattu' and before departing Makkah to return home.

You have now completed your UMRA al-TAMATTU' and you now remove your Ihram. You will stay in Makkah until the **8th of Dhulhijja** when you will go to Arafah.

During your waiting period in Makkah you should spend more time in duas. You can perform as many Tawaaf as you may wish in your ordinary clothes (not in Ihram) for your deceased parents, relatives and friends at the Holy Haram.

Checklist for Items to be Taken to Arafah/Muzdhalifah/Mina by each Hujjaj

• One mussallah (janamaaz) made of straw.

• One bottle of drinking water.

• One (water) spray bottle.

• Cash Saudi Riyals 200 if you have already paid to your group leader for purchasing a Qurbani coupon otherwise, you will require SR500 (children need not carry more than 50 Riyals).

• Sleeping bag or Hajj mat.

• One small powerful torch.

• One folding fan and umbrella for ladies.

• An extra pair of rubber slippers.

• One small pouch to collect pebbles for Shaitaan

• One pair of clothes to be worn after removing the

Ihram on the 10th of Dhulhijja at Munna which is Idd
• One pair of sunglasses, option.

• Snacks like Ghatia, chevda, Khari Puri, cookies, cheese and buns.

Hajj al-Tamattu'

01. Makkah – Ihram & Talbiya
02. Arafah
03. Muzdhalifah
04. Munna - Hitting of the big Shaitaan
05. Munna - Qurbani
06. Munna - Taqseer or Halaq
07. Munna - Mabeet on 10th & 11th Dhulhijja
08. Makkah - Tawaaf of Khan al-Ka'aba
09. Makkah - Two rakaats Salaat for Tawaaf
10. Makkah - Saee'
11. Makkah - Tawaaf-un-Nissa
12. Makkah - Two rakaats Salaat for Tawaaf
13. Munna - Hitting all three Shaitaans on
- the 11th & 12th Dhulhijja

Optional but Highly Recommended

14. Makkah - Tawaaf-ul-Wida
15. Makkah Two rakaats Salaat for Tawaaf

Makkah/Arafah - 8th Dhulhijja

Most of the Hujjaj depart Makkah for Arafah before Maghrib depending on the circumstances. This is the toughest part of Hajj. Most of the groups have air condition buses. In Arafah all Hujjaj stay in tents and Jamaat Salaat, A'amaal, duas and majlisi are organized. No matter, how hard we may plan, things could still go wrong and again the key words here are **"patience and tolerance."**

Sandwiches and drinks served usually by the organizer of your group during your stay in Arafah and Munna if **possible and available.** Therefore, Hujjaj are requested to carry (some snacks) with them in case sandwiches cannot be provided.

All of the above items must fit in the Hajj travelling bag (except for the sleeping bag). Please make sure to keep your cash and your ID card with you at all times.

Hajj al-Tamattu'- 8th Dhulhijja At Makkah

Mustahab Ghusl for wearing the Ihram.

Niyyat: "I am doing Ghusl for wearing Ihram for Hajj al-Tamattu' for Hajje-tul-Islam, Qurbatan Ilallah". Late in the evening you will Inshallah proceed to Arafah and spend the night in duas and A'amaal.

1) 8th Dhulhijja Ihram and Talbiya

You will put your Ihram on at Makkah either at Makam al-Ibrahim, or anywhere in the Holy Haram or at your place of residence, then immediately proclaim Talbiya - and the 25 things become Haraam.

Late in the evening you will proceed to Arafah and spend the night in duas and A'amaal.

During your journey and your stay at Arafah, Muzdhlifah and Munna you should refrain from worldly talks and occupy yourself in remembering Allah (SWT) and to thank Him for his blessings that He has bestowed on you. Also do not forget to pray for your deceased parents, relatives and friends.

2) 9th Dhulhijja - Arafah

Niyyat: "I am staying in Arafah from Dhohar to sunset, for Hajje al-Tamattu', for Hajje-tul-Islam, Qurbatan Ilallah".

Inshallah, A'amaal, Duas, Jamaat Salaat, Ziyarat and Majlis are organized by your group organizer.

3) 9th Dhulhijja – Arafah/Muzdhalifah

Inshallah, late in the evening all Hujjaj will proceed to Muzdhalifah where you will stop and pick up the 70 pebbles for hitting the Shaitaan at Munna.

It is recommended that you pray Maghrib & Isha Salaat here but if your group decides to pray at Arafah before leaving for Muzdhalifah, then you should their instructions.

You will spend the night at Muzdhalifah. Ladies, sick, old people, children and volunteers usually go to Munna after picking the pebbles.

There are two Niyyat, a) is Mustahab and b) is Wajib.
• a) "I am spending this night in Muzdhalifah for

Hajj al-Tamattu' for Hajje-tul-Islam, Qurbatan Ilallah".

• b) "I stay in Muzdhalifah from Subh al-Sadiq to sunrise for Hajj al-Tamattu', for Hajje-tul-Islam, Qurbatan Ilallah".

10th Dhulhijja – Muzdhalifa/Mina

After sunrise, the men Hujjaj will Inshallah cross the border and enter into Munna depending on the traffic your group leader may decide to walk which will take about 45 minutes whereas the bus may take about 5 to 7 hours.

After settling down in your place of residence you will Inshallah proceed to hit the big Shaitaan only, followed by Qurbani (sacrifice of a sheep) and performance of Taqseer or Halaq. The night must be spent in Munna.

4) 10th Zilhajj – Munna

Hitting Of The Big Shaitaan

Niyyat: "I am hitting the big Shaitaan Aqba seven times for Hajj al-Tamattu" for Hajje-tul-Islam, Qurbatan IIallah".

5) 10th Dhulhijja – Qurbani At Munna

Niyyat: "I am doing Qurbani for Hajj al-Tamattu', for Hajje-tul-Islam, Qurbatan, Ilallah".

6) 10th Dhulhijja – Taqseer/Halaq At Munna

Niyyat: "I am doing Taqseer or Halaq (whatever the case may be) for Hajj al-Tamattu' for Hajje-tul-Islam, Qurbatan Ilallah".

7) 10th And 11th Dhulhijja – Mabeet At Munna

You have to spend the nights in Munna. It is known as Mabeet. You can spend the first part of the night or the second part. An A'alem of your group will guide you.

Niyyat: "I am spending the night in Munna for Hajj al-Tamattu", for Hajje-tul-Islam, Qurbatan Ilallah".

Some Hujjaj prefer to return to Makkah on the 10th Dhulhijja after mid-night which is permitted by Shariah and after refreshing themselves at their place of residence in Makkah, they proceed to the Holy Haram to perform the A'amaal of Hajj al-Tamattu' but they must return to Mina on the 11th Dhulhijja before Maghrib in order to hit the three Shaitaans.

A'amaal to be performed in Makkah as under

8) Makkah - Tawaaf-ul Hajj

Niyyat: "I am performing Tawaaf for Hajj al-Tamattu' for Hajje-tul-Islam, Qurbatan Ilallah",

9) Makkah - Salaat of Tawaaf

Niyyat: "I am offering 2 Rakaat Salaat for Tawaaf of Hajj al-Tamattu', for Hajje-tul-slam, Qurbatan Ilallah".

10) Makkah – Saee'

Niyyat: "I am doing Saee' by walking seven times between Safa and Marwa for Hajj al-Tamattu' for Hajje-tul-Islam, Qurbatan Ilallah".

11) 11TH & 12TH Dhulhijja At Munna – Hitting All Three Shaitans on Each Day

It is Wajib on these two days to hit at all the three Shaitaans, each with pebbles seven times. The sequence as shown here must be maintained. The first Shaitaan to be hit at must be OOLA the small one, the one nearer to Mash'ar. The next will ALWUSTA, the middle one, and the last one is AQBA the big one closer to Makkah. For those who have a justifiable excuse, like infirmity or sickness, a Naib must be appointed.

Ladies are allowed to perform this act at night, but they are not permitted to appoint a Naib if they can perform it themselves.

• **First Niyyat:** "I strike Shaitaan of OOLA (small) seven times, for Hajj al-Tamattu', for Hajje-tu--Islam, Qurbatan Ilallah".

• **Second Niyyat:** I strike Shaitaan of WUSTA (middle) seven times, for Hajj al-Tamattu' for Hajje-tu--Islam, Qurbatan, Ilallah".

• **Third Niyyat:** "I strike Shaitaan of AQBA seven times for Hajj al-Tamattu', for Hajje-tul-Islam, Qurbatan Ilallah".

Agha Khui says that the pebbles must hit the old, original part of the structure of Shaitaan or known as Jamarat.

Many Hujjaj prefer to return to Makkah on the morning of 11th Dhulhijja after hitting the three Shaitaans, which is permitted by Shariah and after refreshing themselves at the hotel to proceed to the Holy Haram to perform the A'amaal of Hajj al-Tamatu'. You are required to return to Munna before Maghrib.

12) Makkah - Tawawaaf-un-Nissa

Niyyat: "I am performing Tawaaf for Tawaaf-un-Nissa for Hajj al-Tamattu' for Hajje-tul-Islam, Qurbatan Ilallah'.

13) Makkah - Salaat of Tawaaf

Niyyat: "I am offering 2 Rakaat Salaat for Tawaaf-un-Nissa, Qurbatan Ilallah."

14) Tawaaf-ul-Wida (optional but recommended)

Niyyat: "I am performing Tawaaf-ul-Wida Qurbatan Ilallah".

15) Salat of Tawaaf

Niyyat: "I am offering 2 Rakaat Salaat for Tawaaf-ul-Wida, Qurbatan Ilallah".

Please make sure that all the A'amaal of Hajje-Tamattu' are completed before you depart Makkah.

Mustahab Acts at Arafah

1. To remain in the state of Taharat.

2. To make Ghusl (Mustahab) preferably near the time of Dhohar.
3. To keep the mind frees from worldly thoughts and concentrate on prayers and Duas. The famous A'amaal al-Arafah by Imam Husayn A.S. on this day, is the best. See page 91.
4. To pray Dhohar, immediately followed by Asr, with one Adhaan and two Iqamahs.
5. To remember Allah, thank Him, praise Him and seek forgiveness for your sins.
6. You should spend your time in Tasbeehat and Duas and avoid useless talks.

Mustahab Acts at Muzdhalifah

1. To stay in the middle part of the plain of Mash'ar.

2. To pick 70 pebbles from here for Rami of Jamarat (for Shaitaan).

3. To leave Arafah with clean body and calm mind, proceeding with Istighfar.

4. To travel with ease, causing trouble to no-body. If it is difficult to reach Mash'ar before midnight, do not let your Maghrib and Isha prayers be Qadha. Pray on the way.

5. It is Mustahab to pray Maghrib and Isha on the plains of Mash'ar, with one Adhaan and two Iqamahs, even if one-third of the night away.

6. Duas, prayers, dhikr and all acts of worship are recommended in this night, which you have to spend here. If possible try and pray Salaat al-Shaab.

7. After Fajr Salaat, it is Mustahab to remain in the state of Taharat.

Conditions of Qurbani at Munna

The animal offered for sacrifice may be a camel, a cow, a goat or a sheep. But the conditions are as follows:

1. The animal must not have any defects in it's limbs. It must not be very old, sick or emaciated. If the ears are partly torn or have holes, it would not matter, but if

the ears, horns or testicles have been severed or crushed, it would not be sufficient.

2. The age limit prescribed for animals are as follows:

Camel - must have completed it's 5th year and entered the sixth.

Cows and goats - Must be three years old.

Sheep - must have completed eight months, better still if it has completed one year and entered the second. If the person purposely and knowingly selects a young animal in age than above, his Sacrifice would not be sufficient and acceptable. He has to slaughter again.

3. Every person must offer his own Qurbani. There can

4. be no sharing of funds or animal. Ladies, sick or old people can appoint a Naib.

5. Qurbani must be carried out during daytime, unless there is a fear of security. Agha Khui, had said that if due to change in place, it becomes impossible to slaughter in Munna, one must wait and stay, if one can, even till the end of Dhulhijja to complete the Qurbani in Munna, but if this is not at all possible, then Qurbani outside Munna will be valid.

Conditions of Hitting the Shaitaan

The time for Rami Jamarat (hitting of the Shaitaan) is from sunrise to sunset. Ladies are permitted to hit the Shaitaan during the night. You must strike seven times and each time the pebble must hit the Jamarat. If you miss, you must repeat. Nothing, but pebbles or small stones can be used. Hitting with objects like shoes, tins, etc. is not acceptable.

Haram, or better yet from Mash'ar. Each pebble must be a fresh one; you cannot strike with a pebble that has already been used for Shaitaan.

It is Mustahab that the pebble is small in size, just about the size of a finger head, slightly colored and spotted. It is also Mustahab to be in Wudhu, and to recite "Allahu Akber" with every throw.

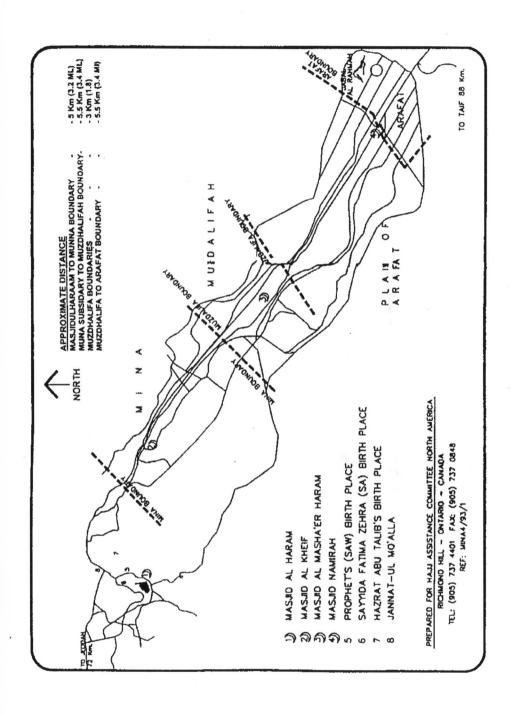

Image:

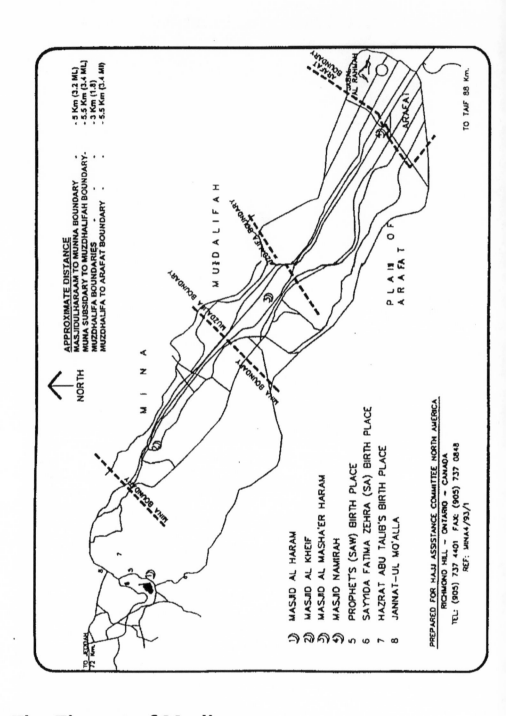

The Ziyarat of Medina

Idhn al-Dukhul means permission to enter the Prophet's mosque for the Ziyarat of the Prophet

O Allah, I am standing at the door of one of the houses of Your Prophet and the family. You have prohibited the people from entering his house except by the permission of Your Prophet and You said: "O You who believe do not enter the house of the Prophet unless permitted to do so". O Allah, I believe in this in his absence just as I believe it in his presence and I know that Your Prophet and Your vicegerents upon whom be peace, are alive in your presence, they are being nourished, they see my position and hear my speech and they return my greetings and (I believe) that You have covered my ears from hearing their speech and have opened the door of perception of their secret conversations (with You); I seek Your permission, O my Lord firstly; then I seek the permission of Your Prophet, peace be upon him and his family secondly and I seek the permission of Your vicegerent, the Imam whose obedience is incumbent upon me and (the permission of) Your angels entrusted over this blessed site thirdly. May I enter, O Prophet of Allah, may I enter O the proof of Allah, may I enter, O angels of Allah who are stationed close to this shrine, so permit me O my master to enter the best of way that You have permitted any of Your friends, if I am not deserving of that then You surely are deserving of that.

Whilst putting your right foot in the Haram read this

In the name of Allah and by Allah in the path of Allah and on the religion of the Prophet of Allah peace be upon him and his family. O Allah forgive me and have mercy on me and turn repentant towards me for You are most forgiving and merciful.

Then say 'Allaho Akber' Allah is greatest 100 times and two Rakaat Namaz with the Niyyat of 'Tahiyat al-Masjid'.

Recited the Ziyarat of the Prophet of Allah as follows:

Peace be upon you, O Messenger of Allah. Peace be upon you, O Prophet of Allah. Peace be upon you, O Muhammad the son of the 'Abd Allah'. Peace be upon you, O seal of the Prophets; I bear witness that you proclaimed the message and established the prayer and paid the zakat and enjoined the good and forbade evil and worshipped Allah with all sincerity until death overtook you; so may the blessings and mercy of Allah be upon you and on your pure family.

Facing the Ka'aba towards the Mimbar Read:

I bear witness that there is no god except Allah. He is unique, there is no partner unto Him and I bear witness that Muhammad is His slave and Prophet.

I bear witness that you are the Prophet of Allah and that you are Muhammad, the son of 'Abd Allah' and I bear witness that you proclaimed the messages of your Lord and that you advised your people and strived in the path of Allah and you served your Lord with wisdom and beautiful preaching until death overtook you; and you fulfilled the duty imposed on you and that you were kind to the believers and severe on the disbelieves. Allah has made you attain the highest position of honour and nobility. Praise be to Allah who, through you, has saved us from polytheism and from going astray; O Allah send Your blessings and the blessings of Your close angels and

Your Messengers and those of Your upright slaves and the people of the heavens and the earth and those who have glorified You, O Lord, from the beginning to the end, on Muhammad Your slave and Messenger and Your Prophet and Your trustworthy and saved one, Your beloved and Your chosen one; Your special, pure and most virtuous one from Your creatures.

O Allah, grant him an elevated status and make him a means to heaven and raise him in a praiseworthy status which the first and the last people will wish to attain. O Allah, You have said: "If they wrong themselves and come to you and seek forgiveness from Allah, and if the Prophet seeks forgiveness for them, they will find Allah forgiving and merciful". I have come to you seeking forgiveness, repenting my sins and I seek your mediation with Allah, who is my Lord and Your Lord that He forgives my sins.

At Maqame Jibra'il, recite the following:

I ask You O generous one, O noble one O close one O distant one that You bestow Your favours on me again.

The Ziyarat of Bibi Fatima Zehra (peace be upon her)

Peace be upon you O daughter of the Prophet of Allah, peace be upon you O daughter of the Messenger of Allah. Peace be upon You O daughter of the beloved of Allah, Peace be upon you O daughter of the friend of Allah, Peace be upon you O daughter of the chosen one by Allah, Peace be upon you O daughter of the trustworthy one of Allah, Peace be upon you O daughter of the best of creation of Allah, Peace be upon you O daughter of the best of the Prophets and Messengers and angels of Allah. Peace be upon you O daughter of the best of creation. Peace be upon you O leader of all women in the world, from the beginning to the end,

Peace be upon you O wife of the friend of Allah and the best of Allah's creation after the Prophet of Allah. Peace be upon you O mother of al-Hasan and al-Husayn, the two leaders of the youths in paradise. Peace be upon you O truthful martyr, Peace be upon you O peaceful and tranquil one. Peace be upon you O excellent and pure one. Peace be upon you O one who has traits of an angel. Peace be upon you O virtuous and pure one;

Peace be upon you O learned one who heard angels speak, Peace be upon you O oppressed one and one whose rights were usurped; Peace be upon you O one who was suppressed and overpowered; Peace, mercy and blessing be upon you O Fatima, the daughter of the Prophet of Allah, May Allah bless you and your soul and body.

I bear witness that you passed away well informed by your Lord and that one who has pleased you has pleased the Prophet of Allah peace be upon him and his family; and one who has displeased you has displeased the Prophet of Allah peace be upon him and his family, and one who has harassed you has harassed the Prophet of Allah peace be upon him and his family and one who establishes links with you establishes links with the Prophet of Allah peace be upon him and his family and one who has cut relations with you has cut relations with the Prophet of Allah peace be upon him and his family because you are part of him and his spirit within him.

I bear witness by Allah and His Prophets and his angels that I am pleased with one whom you are pleased and am angry with one whom you are angry, I dissociate myself from one whom you have dissociated yourself, I befriend myself with one whom you have befriended and am an enemy of one with whom you are an enemy; I detest one whom you detest, I love whom you love, Allah is sufficient as a witness and as one accounting for deeds and as one who repays and rewards.

Recite Salawat followed by two Rakaat Namaaz of Ziyarat and supplicate to Allah:

The Ziyarat of the Imams buried in Janat-ul-Baquee:

Peace be upon you O Imams of guidance, Peace be upon you O people of piety, Peace be upon you O proofs of Allah on the people of the earth; Peace be upon you who were steadfast in dealing with people with justice. Peace be upon you O people of the chosen one.

Peace be upon you the family of the Prophet of Allah, Peace be upon you O people of secret conversations (with Allah), I bear witness that you proclaimed and advised and persevered for the sake of Allah and that you were belied and evil was done to you and you forgave and I bear witness that you are the rightly guided leaders and that obedience to you is incumbent and that your speech is correct and that you invited (to the truth) but were not answered and you commanded but were not followed.

I bear witness that you are the pillars of religion and support of the earth, you were always under the (caring) eyes of Allah who was transferring you from the wombs of the pure ones, the era of ignorance did not contaminate you; the sedition of desires has not partaken of you, you have become pure; your origin is pure.

Through you He has favoured us (with His religion). He has created you in houses in which Allah has allowed His name to be elevated and remembered. He has made our salutations to you to be mercy for us and expiation of our sins for Allah has chosen you for us and has made our creation pure because He has favoured us with your affection.

We are named in front of Him due to your Gnosis and because we acknowledged and believed in you. This is the position of one that has been extravagant and has erred; He has submitted and acknowledged what he has committed and hoped of his sincere position and through you he will be saved from destruction so be my intercessors. I have come to you for the people of the world have turned away from you and have taken the signs of Allah as jest and have become arrogant.

O One who is upright and does not over look; O Eternal One who does not disregard and covers all things You have favoured me with Your help and have shown me the path which You established for me; for Your slaves have turned away from it and have become ignorant of its knowledge and have belittled its rights and have inclined to others; it is Your favour on me with the people that be to You for I am in front of You in this position remembered and subject to (Your) decree so do not deprive me of what I hoped for and, by the sanctity of Muhammad and his pure family, do not disappoint me what I have asked from You, send Your blessings on Muhammad and the family of Muhammad.

Ziyarat of Janab al-Fatima Binte Asad, mother of Imam Ali A.S.

Peace be on the Prophet of Allah, Peace be on the Messenger of Allah, Peace be on Muhammad the leader of the Messengers, Peace be on Muhammad the leader of the foremost ones. Peace be on one whom Allah sent as a mercy to the universe. Peace be on you, O Prophet and the mercy and blessings of Allah be upon you. Peace be on Fatima, the daughter of Asad, the Hashimite, Peace be upon you O truthful and contented one; Peace be upon you O virtuous and pure one; Peace be upon you O virtuous and pure one; Peace be upon You O noble and contented one; Peace be upon you O one who looked after Muhammad, the seal of the Prophets.

Peace be upon you O mother of the leader of the successors. Peace be upon you who showed compassion to the Prophet of Allah, seal of the Prophets; Peace be upon you O one who raised the trustworthy friend of Allah; Peace be upon you, on your soul and on your pure body; May peace, mercy and blessings be upon you and on your son.

I bear witness that you supported in the best manner possible and fulfilled your obligation and strived for the pleasure of Allah and exerted yourself in protecting the Prophet of Allah, being aware of his status; believing in his truthfulness; acknowledging his prophecy, perceiving his blessings; taking responsibility of his upbringing, dealing with him affectionately; ready to serve him; choosing what please him, preferring what he like; I bear witness that you spent your life on the (true) faith and adhering to the most noble religion, being pleased and contented, pure, clean, guarded and virtuous.

May Allah be pleased and satisfied with you; may He make heaven as your house and permanent abode. O Allah, send y our greetings on Muhammad and the family of Muhammad and make my visiting her beneficial to me and make me firm in my love for her and do not deprive me of her intercession and the intercession of the Imams from her loins; so grant me her company and gather me with her and with her pure children;

O Allah, do not make it my last visit to her and grant me another visit to her as long as You keep me alive and if You cause me to die then gather me with her ranks and include me amongst those receiving her intercession by Your mercy, O Most Merciful of the Merciful ones. O Allah, I ask You by her status and high position in front of You, forgive me and my parents and all believing men and women and grant us goodness in this and the next world and save us, by Your mercy, from the punishment of the fire.

The Ziyarat of Hazrat Hamza, the uncle of the Prophet (SA.W) at Ohud:

Peace be upon you O uncle of the Prophet of Allah peace be upon him and his family; Peace be upon you O best of the martyrs; Peace be upon you O lion of Allah and the lion of His Prophet. I bear witness that you fought for Allah, the Most Mighty and Glorious and you exerted yourself and advised the Prophet of Allah and desired (the rewards) available through Allah the Most Glorious.

May my father and mother be sacrificed for you, I have come to you seeking closeness to Allah the Most Mighty and Glorious by visiting you, and seeking nearness to the Prophet of Allah peace be upon him and his family; through that desiring from (your) intercession; seeking from my visiting you freedom of myself and seeking refuge, through you, from the fire; those like me deserve it for the wrong I have done to myself.

(I come) fleeing from my sins which I have committed; fleeing to you hoping g for the mercy of My Lord; I have come to you from a distant land seeking freedom from the fire, my back is loaded with my sins. I have committed what angers my Lord. I did not find anyone more worthy to flee to than you, the Ahl Al-Bayt of mercy, so be my intercessors on the day of my poverty and need. I have traveled to you in a sad state and in distress.

I shed tears in front of you, crying I have come to you lonely; you are amongst those whom Allah has commanded to join with and has urged me towards piety and guided me to His grace and love; He urged me to come to you and inspired me to ask my needs to Him; You are the Ahl Al-Bayt no one befriends you is miserable; one who comes to you is not disappointed and one who is inclined towards You does not lose nor does one who shows enmity towards you become happy.

Recite Two Rakaat Namaaz and say Duas

Ziyarat of Martyrs (Shuhada) of Uhud:

Peace be on the Prophet of Allah, Peace be on the Messenger of Allah; Peace be on Muhammad the son of 'Abd Allah'; Peace be on you, O people of the house of belief and unity; Peace be on you, O helpers of the religion of Allah and helpers of His Prophet and his family, Peace be on you for the patience which you have exercised for what a wonderful abode that is! I bear witness that Allah has chosen you for His religion and chosen you for His Prophet.

I also bear witness that you truly strove for Allah and defended the religion of Allah and His Prophet and you gave yourselves for him. I bear witness that you were killed on the path of the Prophet of Allah so may Allah grant you the best reward of (your services to) His Prophet and for Islam and its followers. May Allah make us see your faces in places of His pleasure and His honour with the Messengers and the truthful ones and the martyrs and the upright ones; for they are the best friends.

I bear witness that you are the party of Allah and that one who wages war against you wages war against Allah. I also bear witness that you are the close, victorious ones to Allah who are living in the proximity of their Lord and are being nourished. May the curse of Allah and the angels and all the people fall on those who killed you.

I have come to visit you, O people of tawhid, knowing your rights and the merits of visiting you seeking closeness to Allah and because of my knowing (your) past honourable deeds and good acts so may the peace, mercy and blessings of Allah be upon you; may the curse, anger and wrath befall on one who killed you O Allah, make my visit to them beneficial to me and make me firm in my resolvement (for them) and make me die (for the same goal) as you made them die and gather me and them in the same abode of your mercy. I bear witness that you have preceded us and we will join you.

When leaving Medina, recite the following Ziyarat Al-Wida'a (farewell Ziyarat) of the Prophet

Peace be upon you O Prophet of Allah I bid you farewell and I ask you (for help) and I send you my salaams. I believe in Allah and in what you have brought and guided me towards. O Allah, do not make it my last visit to the grave of Your Prophet. If You take me away before that I bear witness in my death as I bear witness in my life that there is no god but You and that Muhammad is Your slave and Your Messenger Peace be upon him and his family.

When leaving Jannat-ul-Baquee for the last time, recite this farewell Ziyarat (Ziyarat Al-Wida'a)

Peace be upon you of leaders of guidance, may the mercy and blessings of Allah be showered upon you; I bid you farewell and send you my salutations. We have believed in Allah and in the Prophet and in what you have brought and guided towards.

O my Allah, count us amongst those who bore witness (to this testimony). Peace be on the Prophet of Allah, Peace be on the Messenger of Allah, Peace be on the beloved of Allah, Peace be on the chosen one of Allah, Peace be on the saved one by Allah, Peace be on Muhammad the son of 'Abd Allah', the master and seal of the Prophets and the chosen one by Allah amongst all His creatures on the earth and skies.

Peace be on all His Prophets and Messengers; Peace be on the martyrs and upright prosperous one. Peace be on us and on the upright slaves of Allah. Peace be on you O pure soul; Peace be on you O noble self; Peace be on you, O one with pure descent; Peace be on you, O pure soul, Peace be on you, O son of the best creatures; Peace be on you O son of the chosen Prophet, Peace be on you O son of one sent to all the upright ones; Peace be on you, O son of the bringer of good tidings and warner; Peace be on you, O son of the lamp and light.

Peace be upon you, O son of one supported by the Qur'an; Peace be on you O son of one sent to human beings and Jinns; Peace be on you O son of the bearer of the flag and sign; Peace be on you O son of the intercessor on the day of judgement; Peace be on you O son of one whom Allah drew closer with honour. Peace be on you, and may the mercy and blessings of Allah descent upon you I bear witness that Allah has chosen for you the abode of his blessings before He prescribed His laws or imposed His halal and haraam so he took you towards Him as you were good, pure, contented and purified from all impurity, sanctified from all filth and He has allocated heaven as your resting abode and elevated you to a high station;

May the blessings of Allah be upon you, blessings through which the eyes of His Prophet are delights and his greatest hopes realized. O Allah, send your best, pure and choicest and complete blessings on Your Prophet and Messenger and Your choicest of creatures Muhammad the seal of the Prophets and on the loins of his pure sons and on those succeeding him from his pure family, by Your mercy, O Most Merciful One.

O Allah, I ask You by the right of Muhammad Your chosen one and by Ibrahim, the Progeny of Your Prophet that make my striving to them accepted, due to them, forgive my sins and make my life, due to them, upright and my end, due to them, praiseworthy, my needs, due to them, fulfilled and my actions, due to them pleasing (to You) and my affairs, due to them prosperous and my matters, due to them, commendable.

O Allah, make my success complete, and free me from all troubles and constraints. A Allah, remove Your punishment from me and grant me Your rewards; make me live in Your paradise, grant me Your pleasure and Your safety; include in my upright supplication my parents and my children and all the believers, men and women, those alive or dead, for You are the master of the actions which survive after the doer passes away, A'amin, O Lord of the universe.

Image:

TAWAF GUIDE OF HOLY KAABAH

PREPARED FOR HAJJ ASSISTANCE COMMITTEE - NORTH AMERICA

FAX: (905) 737 0848 TORONTO-CANADA

REF. MECCA.3/93./2

HOLY KAABAH

TAWAF-START HERE

HATIM - GRAVE OF HAZRAT ISMAIL
(HIJR-E ISMAIL)

MAQAM-E IBRAHIM

TAWAF-END HERE

HAJAR-UL ASWAD

N O T E

1 THE MAXIMUM LIMIT/DISTANCE FOR TAWAF OF THE KAABAH IS
40 feet (12 m) PERIMETER
THEREFORE, THE DISTANCE OF TAWAF FROM
HIJR-E ISMAIL IS 9 feet (2.75 m)

2 MAQAM-E IBRAHIM IS OUT OF THE LIMIT FOR TAWAF

3 KEEP AS CLOSE AS POSSIBLE TO THE KAABAH
WITHOUT TOUCHING THE KAABAH, HIJR-E ISMAIL
OR MAQAM-E IBRAHIM

Du'a for Entering Masjid-ul-Haraam

It is better to enter from Bab-ul-Salaam and recite the du'a while near the pillar.

May Peace, mercy and blessings of Allah be upon you O Prophet. In the name of Allah and by Allah, and by what Allah wishes, peace be on the Prophets and Messengers of Allah. Peace be upon the Prophet of Allah (SAW) peace be upon Ibrahim the friend of Allah. Praise be to Allah the Lord of the Universe, In the name of Allah and by Allah and from Allah and to Allah, by whatever Allah wishes and in accordance to the religion of the Prophet of Allah, peace be upon him and his family all the best names belong to Allah, praise be to Allah.

Peace be to the Prophet of Allah, peace be upon Muhammad the son of 'Abd Allah. Peace, mercy and blessings be upon you, O Prophet of Allah. Peace be upon the Prophets and Messengers of Allah. Peace be upon Ibrahim the friend of the Merciful One. Peace be upon the Prophets, praise be to Allah the Lord of the Universe.

Peace be upon us and on the upright slaves of Allah. O Allah send peace on Muhammad and the family of Muhammad and bless Muhammad and the family of Muhammad and have mercy on Muhammad and the family of Muhammad just as You sent peace and blessings and had mercy on Ibrahim and the family of Ibrahim, You are the most Praiseworthy, most Glorious.

O Allah send peace on Muhammad and the family of Muhammad Your slave and Messenger. O Allah send Your blessings on Ibrahim, Your friend and on Your Prophets and Messengers and grant them peace, and peace be upon the Messengers. Praise be to Allah, the Lord of the Universe. O Allah open for me the doors of Your mercy, and make me perform, deeds of Your obedience and pleasure.

Protect me through the protection of faith as long as You make me live, all Praise be to You. Praise be to Allah who has made me amongst His guests and His visitors and amongst those who enlivens His mosques and made me amongst those who converses with Him. O Allah, I am Your slave, visiting Your house; whoever comes and visits there has rights (to ask) and You are the best of hosts, and most noble to visit.

I ask You O Allah, O Merciful One, You are Allah there is no Lord but You; You have no partners You are One, Unique, Independent. You did not beget nor were You begotten nor is there anyone like You; and I bear witness that Muhammad is Your slave and Messenger, peace be upon him and family, O Generous One, O Noble One, O Glorious One, O All-Conquering, O Noble One. I ask You that Your first gift to me of my visiting You be that You grant me freedom from the fire.

Then say this three times:

O Allah, free me from the fire.

And then recite this:

O Allah, increase my sustenance from You, granting me halaal and pure sustenance, remove the evils of Satan amongst the men and jinn, and the evils of the Arabs and the non-Arabs.

Enter the mosque and say as follows:

In the name of Allah and by Allah, on the religion of the Prophet of Allah peace be upon him and his family.

Then face the Khana al-Ka'aba and raise both hands and recite the following:

O Allah, I ask You in my present position and in my first (stages of) of rituals to accept my repentance and overlook my faults and remove my burden. Praise be to Allah who made me reach His sacred sanctuary.

O Allah, I bear witness by You that this is Your sacred sanctuary which You have made a place of return, place of safety and blessing for the people, and a source of guidance for the universe.

O Allah, the slave is Yours, the land is yours, the sanctuary is Yours, I have come seeking Your mercy and I agree to obey You, obeying Your commands, pleased with Your decree. I ask You like a poor person coming to You, scared of Your punishment. O Allah, open the doors of Your mercy for me and me perform deeds of Your obedience and pleasure.

Then invoke the Ka'aba and say this:

Praise be to Allah who has made you great and honoured you and made you noble and a gathering place for the people and a place of safety and blessings, and a source of guidance for the universe.

When you see the Hajr-al-Aswad, say the following:

Praise be to Allah who has guided us to this, had it not been for Allah's guidance, we would not have been guided. Glory be to Allah, praise be to Allah, there is no god but Allah; Allah is the greatest, Allah is greater than His creatures, Allah is greater than what I can be scared and be cautious of. There is no god but Allah, He is unique, there is no partner to Him, to Him belongs the kingdom and praise, He gives life and death, He gives death and life, He is for ever living, He does not die, all goo originates from Him, He is powerful over everything.

O Allah, send peace on Muhammad and the family of Muhammad and bless Muhammad and the family of Muhammad just as you sent peace and blessings and mercy on Ibrahim and the family of Ibrahiim. You are the most praiseworthy and most glorious. And peace be upon all Prophets and Messengers, praise be to Allah, the Lord of the universe. O Allah, I believe in Your promise and attest to Your Prophets and I follow Your book.

After this, keeping the thought of Allah's wrath in mind, slowly proceed forward and on reaching Hajr-al-Aswad raise both hands and praise Allah and send salawat on Prophet Muhammad (SAW) and his Progeny and then recite the following:

O Allah , accept this from me.

If possible, kiss Hajr-al-Aswad; if not, point at it and recite the following:

O Allah, I have fulfilled my trust, and have accomplished my covenant so that You may witness that I have fulfilled my promise; O Allah, in accordance with Your book and the practice of Your Prophet, may Your blessings be sent upon him and his family.

I bear witness that there is no god but Allah, He is unique, there is no partner to Him, and I bear witness that Muhammad is His slave and Messenger, I believe in Allah and disbelieve in Jibt (an idol) and the rebels and al-Lat, al-'Uzza (names of idols) and the worship of Satan and the worship of any rival who is believed in except for Allah.

O Allah, to You I have extended my hands and my need for what You have is great, so accept my glorification (of You) and forgive me and have mercy on me. O Allah, I seek Your protection from disbelief and poverty and (any) situation of disgrace in this world and the hereafter.

Recite the following du'a whilst doing the Tawaaf:

O Allah, I ask You by Your name through which one can walk on the waves of the water just as one can walk on the streets of the earth; and I ask You by Your name through which the feet of Your angels tremble; and I ask you by your name through which Musa supplicated on the mountain of Tur, and You answered him and You showered him with love; and I ask you by Your name through which You have cleansed Muhammad peace be upon him and his family from his past and future accusations; and through which You have completed Your favours on him, I ask You to .....**ask for your needs (Haajat) from Allah and read the following supplication during the Tawaaf:**

O Allah, I am a poor person in front of You, I am scared, asking for protection, do not alter my body (by being disabled) nor change my name (poor reputation).

During the Tawaaf, on reaching the door of the Ka'aba in each round recite this du'a commencing with Salawat:

Your needy person is asking from You, Your poor person and beggar is at Your door, so grant him heaven. O Allah, this is Your house, Your sacred sanctuary, I am Your slave; in this is a position of one who seeks Your protection and refuge from the hell-fire, so free me and my parents and my family and my children and my believing brothers and sisters from the fire, O most Generous and Noble one.

On reaching Hijre Ismail, look up at the (Ka'aba) golden water spout which is at the roof and recite the following du'a:

O Allah, grant me heaven and through Your mercy protect me from the fire and keep me away from sickness, expand (the scope of) my halaal sustenance and remove the evil corruption of the Jinn and men and the evil corruption of the Arabs and the non-Arabs from me.

Recite this du'a when reaching the back of the Ka'aba:

O possessor of favors and power, O most Generous and Noble one, indeed my (good) acts are a few so increase them and accept them from me, for You are the most Hearing, most Knowing.

At Rukn al-Yamani, raising both hands, recite this:

O Allah, O master of health and giver of health and bestower of blessings through health, grant benefits with health to me and to all Your creatures; O Most Merciful and Most kind One of this world and the hereafter; send Your blessings on Muhammad and his family, grant us complete health in its perfect form and the ability to thank You for the health in this world and in the hereafter, O Most Merciful and the Merciful ones.

Then facing the front of the Ka'aba raising both hands say this:

Praise be to Allah who has honoured You and deemed you great, praise be to Allah who sent Muhammad as Prophet and made Ali the Imam. O Allah, guide through him the best of Your creatures and remove from him the evil of Your creatures.

Read the following between Rukn al-Yamani and Hajr-al-Aswad:

O my Lord, grant us virtue in this world and in the hereafter and save us from the punishment of the fire.

In the 7th round at Mustajar (behind the Ka'aba and a little before Rukn al-Yamani), it is recommended to stop a little and spread both hands on the walls of the Ka'aba and, with the face and body touching the wall, recite the following du'a: O Allah, this is Your house, Your slave; in this position I am seeking Your protection from the fire. O Allah, from You is the comfort, relief from suffering and health (comes from You). O Allah, indeed my (good) actions are few so increase them for me and forgive what You know about me which You have hidden from Your creatures, I seek protection by Allah from the fire. O Allah, I have (committed) multitudes of sins and multitudes of slips; You have multitudes of mercy and multitudes forgiveness. O One who answered His most detestablecreatures (Satan) when he said: "Give me respite until the day they are raised", (O Allah), answer me **(ask for your Haajat, confess your sins etc)**.

On reaching Hajr al-Aswad, recite the following:

O Allah, make me contented with what You grant me and bless what You grant me.

After completion of Namaaz al-Tawaaf, say the following:

O Allah, accept this from me, do not make it my last visit from me. All praise and all adoration be to Allah for all His blessings until the praises reach the (level) He loves and is pleased with. O Allah, send Your blessings on Muhammad and his family; accept my (supplications), and purify my heart and make my actions righteous. O Allah, through my obedience to You and Your Messenger, peace be upon him and his family, have mercy on me. O Allah, prevent me from transgressing Your boundaries and make me amongst those who love You and Your Prophet, peace be upon him and his family and on Your angels and the upright slaves.

Then prostrate (do sajda) and recite:

My face has prostrated to You in obedience and submission. There is no god but You, truly, truly, You are the foremost before everything, the last one after everything and I am here in front of You, my forehead is in front of You; so forgive me for no one but You forgives the immense sins; forgive me for I confess my sins against myself, no one can overlook the great sins apart from You.

At the well of Zam Zam, after pouring water on the face and back and drinking it, recite:

O Allah, make it (the water a source) of beneficial knowledge and vast sustenance and cure from every illness and sickness.

After this, perform the Saee' and at Safa facing the Khana al-Ka'aba say 7 times:

Allahu Akbar - (There is no god but Allah)

and say three times:

There is no god but Allah He is Unique, there is no partner unto Him; to Him belongs the sovereignty and praise, He gives life and death, He gives death and life and He is Ever-living, He does not die, and He is powerful over everything.

Then read Salawat three times and read the following du'a also three times:

Allah is the greatest due to His guidance to us, Praise be to Allah for what He has bestowed upon us, Praise be to Allah, the One who is the Ever-existent, the Ever-lasting; Praise be to Allah the Ever-existent, the Eternal-One.

And then say this three times:

I bear witness that there is no god except Allah and I bear witness that Muhammad is His slave and Messenger. We do not worship anyone but Him, sincerely in religion even though the polytheists may hate that. O Allah, I ask you for forgiveness, health and certitude in this world and the hereafter. O Allah, give us virtue in this world and in the hereafter and save us from the hell fire.

Then say 100 times - Allahu Akbar La Ilah Illa Allah

(Allah is Great, there is no god but Allah).

Then say 100 times: Alhamdu Lillah (Praise be to Allah)
Then say 100 times: Subhana'allah (Glory be to Allah)

Then recite this:

There is no god but Allah, the Unique One, He has fulfilled His promise and helped His slave, He has overcome the parties, the Unique one, to Him belongs the kingdom and the praise, the Unique one. O Allah, bless me in death and after death. O Allah, I seek Your protection from the darkness and loneliness of the grave. O Allah, shelter me with the protection of Your throne on the day when there will be shelter except Yours.

Then recite this:

I entrust my religion and myself and family and property and my children to Allah, the most Merciful and Kind. He does not abandon what is entrusted to him. O Allah, make me act according to Your book and practice of Your Prophet and make me die on his religion and protect me from strife.

Then say Allahu Akbar 3 times and recite this du'a:

O Allah, forgive all my sins I have ever committed, if I repeat them then please turn to me in forgiveness again for You are most Forgiving, most Merciful. O Allah, deal with me according to ho You are, for if You deal with me according to how You are You will have mercy on me and if You punish me then You are free from my punishment whereas I am in need of Your mercy.

O One whose mercy I am in need of, have mercy on me and not deal with me according to how I am, for if You deal with me according to how I am You will punish me without being unfair to me. I have become fearful of Your justice, I do not fear Your oppression, O One who is just but does not oppress, have mercy on me. O One who does not disappoint the one who asks Him and does not exhaust His gifts send Your blessings on Muhammad and his family, through Your mercy, save me from the fire.

On the fourth step at Safa facing the Ka'aba recite the following duas:

O Allah, I seek our protection from the punishment of the grave and it's trials and it's strangeness and loneliness and it's darkness and it's narrowness and it's straits. O Allah, shelter me with the shelter of Your throne on the day when there will be no shelter except Yours.

On the bottom step recite:

O Lord of forgiveness, O One who commanded through forgiveness O One who is foremost in forgiveness, O One who rewards through forgiveness, I seek forgiveness, forgiveness, forgiveness, O Most Generous and Noble, O blessings on me again and make me do deeds of obedience and pleasure to You.

When reaching the green pillars of Harwala, recite the following:

In the name of Allah and by Allah and Allah is the greatest, send Your blessings on Muhammad and his family. O Allah, forgive me, have mercy and overlook what You know, for You are most Mighty and Noble and guide me to that which is most firm. O Allah, indeed my (good) acts are few, so increase them for me, and accept them from me. O Allah, for you I strive, my power and strength is due to You, so accept my deeds O You who accept the actions of the pious ones.

When going beyond the second green pillar say the following:

O You who bestow favours and grace, has power, nobility, blessings and generosity; forgive my sins, for no one forgives sins except You.

On reaching the hill of Marwa, recite all the duas which have been mentioned for Safa and recite this du'a too:

O Allah, O one who has commanded through forgiveness, O one who loves forgiveness, O one who gives through forgiveness, O one who forgives through forgiveness, O Lord of forgiveness, I ask for forgiveness, forgiveness, forgiveness.

Whilst crying, recite this throughout the Saee':

O Allah, I ask You to grant me good thoughts of You at all times and pure intention in my depending on You.

For Hajj al-tul Islam On the eve of 8th of Dhulhijja when one leaves for Arafah and when nearing Munna recite the following:

O Allah, I have placed my hopes in You only, I ask from You only, so make me attain my hopes and put my affairs in order.

During the journey, make yourself busy with tasbih and the remembrance of Allah (SWT) and when nearing Arafah recite the following.

O Allah, I have turned to You and I have depended on You and I desire You; I ask You to bless me in my journey and to fulfill my needs and make me amongst those whom You can boast of today in front of those who are better than me.

On the day of Arafah after saying your Dhoharan Salaat on time say whilst facing the Qibla:

Recite Ayatal-Qursi, Salawat, Sura Inna Anzalna, La hawla wala quwwata illa bi'llah and also sura Tawhid. It is recommended to recite each of these 100 times, and together with the duas recommended for the day, recite the following:

Allah is greatest, Praise and Glory be to Allah, and there is no god but Allah. O Allah, I am Your slave so do not make me amongst the disappointed guests. Have mercy on my travelling to You from distant areas. O Allah, the Lord of all holy places, free me from the fire and grant me halaal sustenance and remove the evil corruption of Jinn and human beings from me. O Allah, do not plot against me and do not deceive me and do not test me. O Allah, I ask You by Your power, generosity, nobility and bounties and grace, O best of those who hear, O best of those who see, O quickest in reckoning, O most Merciful of the merciful ones, send Your blessings on Muhammad and his family and do for me [**Raise your both hands and ask for needs**].

A'amal al-Arafah – By Imam Husayn A.S.

Praise belongs to Allah, whose decree none may avert, and whose gift none may prevent. No fashioner's fashioning is like His fashioning, and He is the Generous, the All-embracing. He brought forth the varieties of unprecedented creatures and perfected through His wisdom all He had fashioned. Hidden not from Him are harbingers, nor lost with Him are deposits. He repays every fashioner, feathers the nest of all who are content and has mercy upon all who humble themselves.

He sends down benefits and the all-encompassing Book in radiant light. He hears supplications, averts afflictions, raises up in degrees, and knocks down tyrants. For there is no god other than He, nothing is equal to Him. "Like Him there is naught, and He is the Hearing, the seeing, the subtle, the Aware and He is powerful over all things".

O Allah, I make Thee my quest and bear witness to Thy Lordship and acknowledging that Thou art my Lord and to Thee is my return. Thou created me from dust, then gave me a place in the loins (of my fathers), secure from the uncertainty of Fate and the vagaries of the ages and the years.

I remained a traveler from loin to womb in a time immemorial of past days and bygone centuries. In Thy tenderness, bounty and goodness toward me Thou did not send me out into the empire of the leaders of disbelief, those who broke Thy covenant and cried lies to Thy messengers. Rather Thou sent me out to that guidance which had been foreordained for me, the way, which Thou made easy for me and in which Thou nurtured me. And before that Thou were kind to me through Thy gracious fashioning and abundant blessings.

Thou originated my creation from a sperm-drop spilled and made me to dwell in a threefold gloom among flesh, blood and skin. Thou gave me not to witness my creation, nor did Thou entrust me with anything of my own affair. Then thou sent me out into the world for the guidance that had been foreordained for me, complete and unimpaired. Thou watched over me in the cradle as an infant boy, provided me with food, wholesome milk, and turned the hearts of the nursemaids towards me. Thou entrusted my upbringing to compassionate mothers, guarded me from the calamities brought by the jinn and kept me secure from excess and lack.

High art Thou, O Merciful! O Compassionate! Then when I began to utter speech Thou completed for me Thy abundant blessings. Thou nurtured me more and more each year until, when my nature was perfected and my strength balanced, Thou made Thy argument incumbent upon me by inspiring me with knowledge of Thee, awing me with the marvels of Thy wisdom, awakening me to the wonders of Thy creation which Thou had had multiplied in Thy Heaven and Thy earth, and instructing me in Thy thanks and remembrance. Thou made incumbent upon me Thy obedience and worship, made me to understand what Thy messengers had brought and made easy for me the acceptance of Thy good pleasure. Thou were gracious to me in all of this, through Thy succour and kindness. Then, since Thou created me from the best soil, Thou were not satisfied, my God, that I should have one blessing without another. Thou provided me with varieties of sustenance and kinds of garments and Thy tremendous - most tremendous - graciousness to me and Thy eternal goodness toward me.

And finally, when Thou had completed for me every blessings and turned away from me all misfortunes, Thou were not prevented by my ignorance and audacity from guiding me toward that which would bring me nigh to Thee or from giving me success in that which would bring me close to Thee.

For if I prayed to Thee Thou answered, if I asked of Thee Thou gave, if I obeyed Thee Thou showed Thy gratitude, all of that was to perfect Thy blessings upon me and Thy goodness toward me. So glory be to Thee, Glory be to Thee, who are Producer and Reproducer, Laudable, Glorious Holy are Thy Names and tremendous Thy bounties. So which of Thy blessings, my God, can I enumerate by counting and mentioning? For which of Thy gifts am I able to give thanks? Since they, O lord, are more than reckoners can count or those who entrust to memory can count or those who entrust to memory can attain by knowledge. But the affliction and hardship, O God that Thou turned and averted from me is more than the health and happiness that came to me.

And I witness, my God, by the truth of my faith, the knotted resolutions of my certainty, my pure and unadulterated profession of Unity, the hidden inwardness of my consciousness, the places to which the streams of light of my eyes are attached, the lines on my forehead's surface, the openings for my breath's channels, the parts of my nose's soft point, the paths of my ears' canals.

What my lips close upon and compress, the movements of my tongue in speaking, the joining at the back of my mouth and jaw, the sockets of my molar teeth, the place where I swallow my food and drink, that which bears my brain, the hollow passages of my neck's fibers, that which is contained in my breasts' cavity, the carriers of my aorta, the places where my heart's curtain is attached, the small pieces of flesh around my liver, that which the ribs of my sides encompass, the sockets of my joints, the contraction of my members, the tips of my fingers, my flesh, my blood, my hair, my skin, my nerves, my windpipe, my bones, my brain, my veins, and all of my members, what was knitted upon them in the days when I was a suckling baby, what the earth has taken away from me, my sleep, my waking, my being still, and the movements of my bowing and prostrating, that had I taken pains and had I striven for the duration of the epochs and ages - were my life to be extended through them - to deliver thanks for one of Thy blessings, I would not have been able to do so, except by Thy grace, which alone makes incumbent upon me never-ending and ever-renewed gratitude to Thee, and fresh and ever present praise.

Indeed, and were I and the reckoners among Thy creatures ever so eager to calculate the extent of Thy bestowal of blessings, whether past or approaching, we would fail to encompass it through numbers or to calculate it's boundaries. Never! How could it ever be done! For Thou announce in Thy eloquent Book and truthful Tiding, Thy Book, O God, Thy Message, has spoken the truth! And Thy prophets and messengers delivered Thy revelation that Thou had sent down upon them and the religion that Thou had promulgated for them and through them.

And I witness, my God, my effort, my diligence, and the extent of my obedience and my capacity, and I say as a believer possessing certainty, "Praise belongs to God, who has not taken to Him a son" that He might have an heir, "and who has not any associate in His dominion" who might oppose Him in what He creates, "nor any protector out of humbleness" who would aid Him in what He fashions. So glory be to Him, glory be to Him!

"Why, were there gods in earth and heaven other than God, they would surely go to ruin" and be rent. Glory be to God, the Unique, the One, "the Everlasting Refuge" who " has not begotten, nor has He been begotten, and equal to Him there is none" Praise belongs to God, praise equal to the praise of the angels stationed near to Him and the prophets sent by Him. And God bless His elect, Muhammad, the Seal of the Prophets, and his virtuous, pure and sincere household, and give them peace.

Namaz al-Shab

It can be prayed anytime after midnight (Midnight is the exact half between sunset and sunrise). It is better and more preferable to pray during the last hours of the night and just before dawn so that one can stay awake and pray morning prayers before retiring.

Short Way of Praying Namaz al-Shab

There are a total of 11 rakaats in Namaz al-Shab.
Start with praying 8 rakaats i.e. 4 prayers of 2 rakaats each like the subh prayer to be prayed with the Niyat of

Salaat al-Shab. In both the rakaats recite Sura al-Hamd followed by any other Sura. Then recite 2 rakaats with the Niyyat of **Salaat al-Shafa, which** is to be prayed like the morning prayer. After that pray 1 rakaat Salaat with the Niyyat of **Salaat al-Witr.** It is prayed like the second rakaat of Salaat al-Subh. This one rakaat is the most important of the whole Salaat al-shab. Details of how to pray are described.

How To Pray Salaat al-Witr:

Take Tasbeeh in your hand and stand up. Make Niyyat of salaat al-witr, say Takbeer and recite Sura al-Hamd followed by Sura al-Qul-Huwallahu-Ahad three times then

Sura al-Qul-Audhu Bi-Rabbil Falaq and Sura al-Qul-Audhubi-Rabbin-Naas each once.

Qunuut

Then say Takbeer and raise your hands for Qunuut in which any Dua may be recited. It is preferable to recite the following Dua.

"Lailaha Illalahul Haleemul Kareem; Lailaha Illalaahul Aliyyul Adheem; Subhanallahi Rabbi--Samawaati-s-Sab'e, Wa Rabbil Aradheena-s-Sab'-e; Wamaa Feehinna Wamaa Baina-Hunna; Wa Rabbil Arshil Adheem; Wal Hamdulillahi Rabbil Aala Meen; Waswallalahu Alaa Muhammadin Wa Aalheit Twaahereen."

Then hold the Tasbee in your right hand for counting and raise your left hand pray for **40 Momineen and Mominaat** whether dead or alive in the following manner:

"Allahum-Maghfirli and the name of the Momineen or Mominaat".
Then recite 100 times **"Astagh-Firul-Laha Rabbi Wa Atuubu Ilayh"**

Then recite 7 times: **"Hadha Maqaamul Aaedheebeka Minan-Naar".**

After that recite 300 times. **"Alafv"**.

Finish the prayer in the usual way by going into Rukuu and Sajdah followed by Tashahud and Salaam. After finishing recite Tasbee al-Fatima Zehra A.S. Then make Sajda al-Shukr.

Ziyarat of Shaam

Please refer to page numbers 5 to 14, which are very important except for a few changes for Ziyarat in Syria, which are mentioned below.

Information For Syrian Visa

They are very strict especially Zuwars holding Tanzanian, Kenyan, Ugandan, Indian, Pakistani and Shri Lankan passports.

You must obtain your Visa from the country of your residence before you proceed to Syria. If you are going to go to Iran then please make sure that you have a multiple visa for Syria otherwise you will have a problem on your return from Iran.

If you have joined a group then your group organizer will be responsible for obtain your visa.

Hotels & Restaurants

In addition to five star hotels mentioned in this booklet, there are also many 2 and 3 star hotels at the city centre, known as the MERGE which are less expensive and affordable.

There are also many restaurants at the MERGE but we will recommend two, ALI BABA and ABU KAMAL the food is also very reasonable.

Transportation

Taxis are very cheap in Damascus. From the city centre to Raudhah of Bibi Zainab may cost you about Fifty Syrian Pounds.

Traveller's Cheques

It is very difficult to cash your traveler's cheques and we advise you to carry US Dollars bills in large denomination.

Currencies

There is an exchange control in Syria and Zuwars are advised not to cash their currency in stores but to go to the banks. It is difficult to cash Traveler's cheques and we recommend you carry US Dollars bills with you in large denomination for better rate. If you have joined a group then the group leader can assist you in exchanging your currency. Exchange only what you think you will need. You will not be able to reconvert the Syrian Pounds into US Dollars.

The rate of exchange fluctuates against the American Dollar and the rate in December 1997 was about 35/40 Syrian Pounds to one US Dollar.

Weather

During the months of December, January and February are very cold and you will require thermal undergarments, winter coat and winter gloves.

March, April, August, September and October and are pleasant months.

June and July are very hot.

Damascus – Raudhah of Bibi Zainab A.S.

You will visit the Raudhah of Bibi Zainab A.S. in the town of As-Sayyida Zainab. Bibi Zainab A.S. was the daughter of our first Imam Hazrat Ali A.S. and Bibi Fatima Zehra A.S.

She was born in Medina on 1st Shabaan in the year 6 A.H. and she died in the year 62 A.H. When she was born, the Holy Prophet (Saw) gave her the name of 'Zainab' by the order of the Almighty Allah (SWT). Bibi Zainab A.S. was a very clever, intelligent and pious lady. She devoted her whole life in spreading and saving Islam. She used to teach Quraan with the meanings to the ladies of Kufa. Imam Zainul Abedeen A.S.'s mother died when he was very young and Bibi Zainab A.S. used to take care of him. In the year 60 A.H. she went with Imam Husayn .A.S. to Karbala'. On every occasion in Karbala', Imam Husayn A.S. used to take the advice of Bibi Zainab A.S. On the day of Ashura, her two sons, Ibrahim and Aun Muhammad sacrificed their lives for the sake of Islam. On the 11th Muharram, 60 A.H. they were taken captives and marched through the towns of Kufa and Shaam.

For one year they stayed captives in Damascus. Bibi Zainab A.S. faced Yazid after the Tragedy of Karbala' and told him of the wrongs he had done. She also gave very good lectures whenever she got a chance, she therefore enabled the people to know the principles and practices of Islam and the wrong and merciless killings of the followers of Imam Husayn A.S. in Karbala' by Yazid and his army. Due to her honesty, bravery and truthfulness, Islam spread through Shaam.

When they were released from prison, she, along with the rest of the members of Ahlul Bayt went to Medina. Even in Medina, she continued preaching. Islam spread rapidly. The governor of Medina became very frightened and wrote to Yazid that Bibi Zainab A.S. was in Medina and was spreading Islam quickly and that she would break his empire. Yazid gave orders that Bibi Zainab A.S. should leave Medina and settle in a village outside Medina. Later on from there she was sent to a town called Misar which is in Egypt.

She continued spreading Islam there as well. Yazid became very scared so he once again ordered that she be taken prisoner and brought to Shaam. When she arrived at a small village on the boundary of Shaam, she remembered where Imam Husayn A.S. head had been kept on a farm under a tree. When she found the tree, she started crying.

A man of Shaam, who was a follower and friend of Yazid, saw her and hit her with a spade on her head. She collapsed and died. Imam Zainul Abedeen A.S. buried her there. That is how this small town came to be known as As-Sayyid Zainab. According to historians, Bibi Zainab's A.S. husband - Abdullah Ibnne Ja'far at-Tayyar was a very rich man. He bought the surrounding land and made the Raudhah especially in the name of Bib Zainab A.S.

In the town of Misar in Egypt, there is another Ziyarat of Bibi Zainab and the place is known as Masjid al-Zainabia. This Bibi Zainab is the daughter of Yahya, Yahya binte Zayed, Zayed Binte Zainul Abedeen. She is the great granddaughter of our 4th Imam Zainul Abedeen A.S. The Bohoras go to Cairo to the Ziyarat of this Bibi Zainab.

Hajar Bin Udai And His Sons

He was the companion of our Prophet of Islam (SAW) and Hazrat Imam Ali A.S. He was the Commander-in-Chief of Imam Ali's army in the battle of Siffeen. He, together with his sons and other people, was sent by Imam Ali A.S. to see Moaviya on a special project. At the border he was recognized and was arrested along with his people including his two sons. Moaviya asked them to renounce their allegiance to Imam Ali A.S., but they refused and stood steadfast in their faith for Imam Ali A.S., They were killed. He witnessed his two sons being killed. They are buried here. This place is known as MAKAME ADRA, which is about 40 km from the city.

It is narrated that Bibi Zainab A.S. has said that 'anybody who comes for my Ziyarat and does not perform the Ziyarat of Hajar Bin Udai then his/her Ziyarat is incomplete.

Raudhah of Hazrat Janab al-Ruqayya A.S.

She was the young daughter of Imam Husayn A.S. She was also present in Karbala'. (From Karbala' along with the rest of the family of Imam Husayn A.S.) she was taken prisoner and taken to Shaam. It is here that she passed away.

Raudhah of Bibi Kulthum A.S.

She was the sister of Imam Husayn A.S. She was born in 7 A.H. and died in 62 A.H. She was the youngest daughter of Bibi Fatima A.S. She was also taken prisoner and brought to Shaam along with the others. When Bibi Zainab A.S. was martyred, Bibi Kulthum A.S. was with her in Shaam. She used to live in Shaam and it is here that she passed away and is buried. Her husband's name was Mohamed Ibne Ja'far at-Tayyar who was the brother of the husband of Bibi Zainab A.S., but he passed away before the incident of Karbala'.

Raudhah of Bibi Umm al-Salma Wife of Our Prophet of Islam (Saw)

She was the wife of the Holy Prophet (SAW). She used to love the children of Bibi Fatima A.S. The Holy Prophet (SAW) had already told her about the death of Imam Husayn .A.S and the incident of Karbala'. When Imam Husayn A.S. was killed in Karbala', Umm al-Salma saw the Holy Prophet in her dream and she told him that his grandson, Imam Husayn A.S. had been martyred. The first majlis of Imam Husayn A.S. (and his sacrifice) was conducted by Umm al-Salma in Medina. She used to cry a lot when recalling the incident of Karbala' and one year later she passed away. In Makkah, when Bibi Khadija A.S. passed away, the Holy Prophet (SAW) kept her with Bibi Fatima A.S. Umm al- Salma used to say that Bibi Fatima A.S. had a lot of knowledge and did not need to learn anything but instead Umm al-Salma learned a lot from her.

Raudhah of Bibi Fizza A.S.

She was the daughter of a king in Ethiopia. She left her father and went to work as a maid of Janab al-Fatima Zehra A.S. She was only 11 years of age when she came to serve Bibi Fatima A.S. It is believed that she knew how to make gold and she also knew the Holy Quran by heart. Once she invited the Ahlul Bayt for dinner and with her dua, the food was sent to her from Heaven by the order of Allah (SWT).

After the death of Bibi Fatima A.S. she continued to stay with the Ahlul Bayt, even though she had sons who were very rich. Imam Husayn A.S. even took her to Karbala'. On every occasion in Karbala', she was with Bibi Zainab A.S. Imam Husayn A.S. respected her very much. She died in Shaam and is buried there.

It is said that when Yazid was misbehaving in the Darbar of Shaam against the Ahlul Bayt A.S. When she stood in front of Bibi Zainab A.S. Yazid gave ordered that Bibi Fizza should whipped. Bibi Fizza came forward and gave a daring speech addressing the African slaves who were the bodyguards. She told them it was a shame on them that in their presence Yazid was ordering her to be whipped. The slaves were very much affected by her speech and they immediately turned towards Yazid and told him that if Bibi Fizza was whipped they would attack with their swords already drawn. Yazid ordered the slaves to stop.

Raudhah of Janab al-Abdullah Ibne Ja'far at-Tayyar A.R.

He was the son of Janabe Ja'far at-Tayyar and the grandson of Janabe Abu Talib and Bibi Fatima Binte Asad. He was the husband of Bibi Zainab A.S. he was a very rich and a successful businessman. He used to help the poor and needy from far and wide. Everyday, he used to have guests at his place. After the death of Bibi Zainab A.S. he continued living in Shaam and it is here that he passed away.

Raudhah of Obais Ibne Kaab A.R.

He was the husband of Bibi Halima and was a resident of Makkah. When the Holy Prophet (SAW) was five years old, he stayed in Makkah with Obais. Later he came with the Holy Prophet (SAW) to Medina and embraced Islam. At that time, He used to live in Shaam and passed away here. This Raudhah has since been closed.

Raudhah of Hazrat Bilal A.R. – Moazzin

He was a resident of Ethiopia. He was a slave when he first came to Makkah. The Holy Prophet (SAW) bought him and then freed him from slavery. The Prophet of Islam used to love him very much and used to treat him like a brother.

In Medina in the year 1 A.H., they built the Masjid and called it Masjid al-Nabawee and Hazrat Bilal used to give Adhaan there. In the year 8 A.H. he was ordered by the Prophet of Islam to climb on the top of Khan al-Ka'aba and give Adhaan. Hazrat Bilal used to love the Prophet (SAW) very much so after the death of the Prophet of Islam he migrated to Shaam. One night Hazrat Bilal saw the Prophet of Allah (SAW) in his dream. The Prophet asked Bilal "why did you leave our home"? So Hazrat Bilal returned to Medina.

He went to pay his respect to Bibi Fatima A.S. who asked him to please recite Adhaan. Bilal agreed at once and as soon as he started the Adhaan, Bibi Fatima A.S. fainted. She remembered her father, the Prophet of Islam. Bibi Fizza went immediately to Hazrat Bilal and asked him to stop the Adhaan because Bibi Fatima A.S. had fainted.

He returned to Shaam because the people of Medina used to bother Hazrat Ali A.S. and Bibi Fatima

A.S. and Hazrat Bilal felt very badly. Bilal passed away in Shaam.

Raudhah of Hazrat Abdulla Ibne Imam Zainul Abedeen A.S.

He was the son of our 4th Imam. He migrated from Medina and came to live in Shaam. He was the grandson of Imam Hassan A.S., his mother was the daughter of Imam Hassan A.S. He was a very brave, clever and religious man and used to a lot of 'ibadat'. He was the younger brother of our 5th Imam - Imam Mohamed Baqir A.S. He passed away in Shaam and is buried there.

Raudhah of Bibi Fatima Sughra Binte Imam Husayn A.S.

She was the daughter of Imam Husayn A.S. Due to the fact that she was very ill, she was unable to go to Karbala' with her father. It was when Bibi Zainab A.S. was taken prisoner the second time and taken to Shaam that Bibi Fatima Sughra went with her, it was here in Shaam that she passed away. **This Raudhah has since been closed.**

Ganje Sar al-Shohada al-Karbala'

This is situated in the compound of the Ummayad mosque. This is the place where the heads of the Martyrs of Karbala' were kept. In the year 60 A.H. Yazid released the members of the Ahlul Bait from the prison, according to one historian, Imam Zainul Abedeen A.S. buried all the head of the martyrs of Karbala' Here. According to another historian it is said that he went to Karbala' and buried them there. Altogether there are 16 heads here including Hazrat Hur's.

Musalla of Imam Zainul Abedeen A.S.

This is situated just outside Sar al-Shohada and it is narrated that the Imam prayed here before he took the heads to Karbala'.

This place is locked but if you are lucky the guard may open it for you and you can say your two rakaats Salaat.

Place where they imprisoned the 4th imam

According to one historian, Imam Zainul Abedeen A.S. was imprisoned separately by Yazid.

Raudhah of Bibi Sakina Binte Imam Husayn A.S.

She was the daughter of Imam Husayn A.S. and the sister of Ali Asghar A.S. Her mother's name was Umme Rubab. Bibi Sakina had gone to Karbala' with Imam Husayn A.S. She faced severe hardship after the tragedy of Karbala'. She was also taken prisoner with the rest of Imam Husayn's family and taken to Kufa and then to Shaam. Yazid Maloon tied her neck and she was also slapped.

She died when she was sill in prison and was first buried in the prison near Bani Ummayad but after many years, one A'alem, saw Bibi Sakina A.S. in his dream. She asked him to remove her body from the grave and bury her elsewhere because water was seeping in her grave. So, with the advise of other A'alems, the man had the grave opened. They saw that indeed the water was filling the grave. When they brought the body out the grave they found it to be intact. The A'alem held the body in his hands till another grave was dug at another location and buried her there and the Raudhah is now known as Bibi Ruqaya A.S.

Place Where Bibi Zainab A.S. Gave Khutba

This is in the courtyard of the Ummayyad mosque or Jami Amawi where Yazid used to hold his court and give his orders.

Well of Prophet Hood A.S.

Prophet Hood A.S. was the next Prophet after Hazrat Nuh A.S. He was a very handsome man. He was 6 feet tall. He preached for many years but the people of that time were very wild. They refused to listen to him and to believe in Allah. At last Allah (SWT) punished them.

All the mountains turned in sand. The people turned into stones and were buried beneath the sand. After thousands of years by the order of Mansur Dawaniki, during the time of our 7th Imam, a well was dug in this place. But instead of water, they found stones in the shape of human beings. Mansur Dawaniki and the other people were very surprised. They went to our 7th Imam, Imam Musa al-Kadhim A.S. and asked him about this . Our Imam revealed that these are the people of Hood and because they disobeyed Allah (SWT), He punished them by turning them into stones.

Mimber of Imam Zainul Abedeen A.S.

This mimber is in the Masjid al-Bani Ummaya where Yazid used to hold his orders. This is what we call DARBAR al-SHAAM. It was here that the members of Ahlul Bayt were held captive and Yazid used to mistreat them and ask them all types of questions.

One day, Imam Zainul Abedeen A.S. got a chance to give a sermon. He climbed on the Mimber and narrated the true story of how Imam Husayn A.S. and his followers were martyred and how Yazid used to mistreat them. Our 4th Imam preached the sermon in such a way that all the people present in Yazid's court started to cry. When Yazid saw that it was getting out of hand, he gave an order for Adhaan and stopped the Imam from preaching. This is why this Mimber is known as Mimber al-Imam Zainul Abdedeen A.S.

Musalla of Prophet Khizer A.S.

Allah (SWT) has given him a stick with a lot of Barkat (blessings). If he puts the stick in the water, it will become a ship and if he puts it in the earth, it will turn into a fruit-bearing tree. Prophet Khizer A.S. came into the world 300 years before Prophet Issa A.S. and he is still alive today. He has visited al the Imams and greeted them with salaams. He also goes and greets our 12th Imam, Hazrat Mahdi Sahebuz Dhaman A.S. now and then. It is narrated the he will re-appear with our 12th Imam A.S.

Allah (SWT) has given Prophet Khizer a gift he touches a dry stick or plant with his hands, it at once turns green.

Raas ul-Husayn A.S.

This is the place where the head of Imam Husayn A.S. was kept.

Raudhah of Prophet Yahya Bin Zakaria A.S.

Prophet Yahya A.S. was martyred due to the lies of one sinful woman and his head was kept in the same place where the head of Imam Husayn A.S. was kept.

A Fourteen Hundred Year Old Door in Bazar Of Shaam Knonw A. S. "Bab al-Faraj"

It is from this door that the members of Ahlul Bayt entered when they were taken to Shaam. They had to wait for 36 hours so that the court could be decorated before they entered.

Ziyarat of Iran

Please refer to page numbers 05 to 14, which are very important except for a few changes to Ziyarat in Iran which, are mentioned below.

Information for Iran Visa

You must obtain your Visa from the country of your residence before you proceed to Iran. If you are going to go to Iraq from Iran then please make sure that you have a multiple visa for Iran otherwise you will have problem on your return from Iraq. If you have joined a group then your group organizer will be responsible for obtaining your Visa.

Hotels & Restaurants

In addition to five stars hotels mentioned in this booklet, there are also many 2 and 3 star hotels at the city centre, and they are affordable. There is also a Pilgrims House managed by the Kanji family.

Transportation

Taxis are very cheap in Iran.

Traveller's Cheques

It is very difficult to cash your traveler's cheques we advise you to carry US Dollars bills in large denomination.

Currencies

There is exchange control in Iran and Zuwars are advised not to cash their currency in stores but to go to the banks. It is difficult to cash Traveler's cheques and we recommend you carry US Dollars bills with you in large denomination for better rate. If you have joined a group then the group organizer can assist you in exchanging your currency.

Exchange only what you think you will need. You will not be able to reconvert the Iranian Riyals or Tumans into US Dollars.

The rate of exchange fluctuates against the American Dollar and the rate in December 1997 was about 350/400 Iranian to one US Dollar.

Weather

Temperatures vary considerably from season to season and from one place to another. During the months of December, January, February and March are very cold and you will require thermal undergarments, winter coat and winter gloves.

March, April, August, September and October and are pleasant months.

June and July are very hot.

Every Monday and Thursday there is a flight by AIR IRAN to Teheran Mehrabad International Airport, which is about 7 km away from the city.

The flight departs Damascus late in the evening and arrives in Teheran at about 11:00 PM. Make sure before you depart Damascus that you have a confirmed ticket Teheran/Mashad/Teheran otherwise you will have a lot of problem.

If you have joined a group then the organizer of your group will take care of everything.

After clearing Immigration and customs you will proceed to your hotel and rest for the night.

You are required to declare the following, and if you do not then at the time of your arrival (you may get into trouble when leaving Iran).

Import Into Iran

1. There is no restriction of the Foreign Currency but the amount must be declared upon arrival at the airport.

2. All Video and camera equipment must be declared.

Export Allowances

1. Every passenger may take one hand-woven carpet or two rugs (a maximum size of 12 sq. m) provided that they are not antiques.

2. Every passenger may, when departing the country, carry 150 grams of wrought gold without gems and upto 3 kgs of wrought silverware without gems.

Our experience tells us that you should include the following items in your list of souvenirs. Saffron, pistachio, different kinds of pastries, nuts, dates, gems like aqeeq, feeroza, dur al-najaf and other. Also all kinds of Tasbih and small decorative placements where you would keep your sajdagha when saying your Salaat.

Teheran/Qum

The next day early in the morning you should proceed to Qum to visit the Raudhah of Janabe

Masuma Fatima Binte Imam Musa al-Kadhim A.S. and the sister of Imam Ridha' A.S. On your way back to Teheran you should visit Masjid al-Jumkaran, Mazaar of Imam Khomeini and Bashete Zahra.

Qum – Raudhah Of Janab al-Masuma Fatima Binte Imam Musa al-Kadhim A.S.

She was the daughter of our 7th Imam, Imam Musa al-Kadhim A.S. and the sister of Imam Ali Ridha' A.S. Her mother's name was Ummul Banin Najma. The meaning of Qum is to "stand" as the ship of Nabi Nooh A.S. had stopped here. It is said that our 12th Imam A.S. will start Jehad from here.

The Holy Prophet (SAW) said 150 years before the death of Masuma al-Qum one of his daughter would be buried in Qum, where many Mujtahids and A'alems will be ready to preach.

After the departure of Imam Ridha' A.S. from Medina, she missed his brother so much that she decided to go to Mashad also known as Khorasan to meet him. When she arrived Qum, which is on the way to Mashad, she got the news that the Imam had been poisoned and had died.

She was very upset and became ill. Within 40 days of the death of the Imam, she passed away in Qum. When she was buried, they found her grave had already been dug. Two men came with Nikab (covered faces) and led Namaaz al-Janaaza and buried her. Our 7th Imam A.S. is recorded to have said that before visiting him in Mashad you should first visit his sister in Qum, and that who ever visits her shall enter Jannat.

Masjid al-Jumkaran

Hassan Bin Maslah by the order of our 12th IMAM HAZRAT MAHDI A.S built this Masjid. The Imam has said that to pray four rakaat Salaat in this Masjid is equal to the thawab of praying inside Khan al-Ka'aba.

It is narrated that Imam Mahdi A.S. visits this Masjid every Tuesday night. There is a well behind this Masjid and Zuwar write AREEZA asking the Imam to take their Haajat to Allah (SWT) and they put it in this well.

Sheikh Saleh (Hassan Maslah Jamkarany) narrates in his book that one Thursday night eve 17th of Ramadhan, and he was sleeping in Jamkaran site (small village) when suddenly he heard someone knocking at the door. He opened it and saw a couple of Sheikhs (clergymen) who after saluting him asked him to follow them, telling him that his master wanted to see you. He went with them to a place, where Masjid al-Jumkaran (now stands). He saw a throne and a very nice carpet on the floor and a young man of about 30 years of age sitting on it and he was informed that he (the person sitting on the throne) was our 12th Imam A.S. An old man was sitting beside him and was reading a book and more than 60 people in green and white robe were praying around the throne. Later on, he was made to understand that the old man was Nabi Khizr A.S.

Our Imam called Sheikh Saleh by his name and told him to tell the people that they were planting on land, which was not just for planting. They had to pay back all the profit they made from the crops and that with the proceeds they were to build a Masjid on this land. This is a very sacred land and Allah (SWT) picked it from all others.

Sheikh Saleh told the Imam that the people would not believe him and the Imam should give him some sign or a letter. The Imam replied that some kind of a sign at the site would be put till the people would accept his message.

So, go and deliver my message to them to build the Masjid from "ardeha" funds from our private property. Tell the people that this is a very sacred place of they should recite four rakaats Salaat. Two rakaats with the Niyyat of "Tahiyat al-Masjid" and the other two rakaats are for "Imam al-Dhamana A.S." The Imam further said that each person that recite these four rakaats will get the thawab of reciting inside the Khan al-Ka'aba.

The Imam further said that among the sheep of "Jaafar Kashany", a shepherd, there is a black and white sheep, which Sheikh Saleh must buy and sacrifice on this land and then distribute the meat among the sick and the poor Allah (SWT) will then heal. He further writes in his book that he returned to his house but could not get any sleep and was thinking until morning. After Salaat al-Fajr he immediately went to the place the Imam had mentioned and found that a boundary of chains had already been put around the land and that was the sign of the area.

Sheikh Saleh further writes that he then went to Qum and when reaching the house that he was asked to visit, he met a man waiting for him at the door and said to him that his master had been waiting to see him since Fajr. He was escorted inside the house and after exchanging salaams the Sayyid then asked Sheikh Saleh whether his name was Hassan Maslah, to which he replied yes. He told me that he dreamed last night that he will be coming to see him and whatever he was asked in his dream he should act accordingly. Sheikh Hassan Maslah, repeated his whole dream and after we went towards the land designated for the Masjid, we saw Jaafar Kashany the shepherd and among his flock of sheep we saw the white and black sheep who was at the end of the flock. The shepherd swore that he had never seen that sheep before in his flock and how hard he tried to catch he was not able.

Sheikh Hassan Maslah Jamkarany said the sheep came to him as if it knows him for years. He caught it and sacrificed it on the land and distributed the meat as per instructions in his dream.

The Masjid was then erected and the chains that were around the plot was removed and taken to Qum. The sick used to visit him and rub their bodies against the chains and they would be healed.

After the death of Sheikh Hassan Maslah Jamkarany all the chains disappeared.

Teheran – Ziyaraats

Raudhah of Shah Abdul Azim

He was the great grandson of Imam Hassan A.S.

Raudhah of Imamzada Saleh Bin Imam Moosa al-Kadhim A.S.

He was the brother of Imam Ridha' A.S.

Raudhah of Janabe Hamza Bin Abul Qasim Ibne Imam Moosa al-Kadhim A.S.

He was the grand son of Imam Musa al-Kadhim A.S.

Raudhah of Sayyed Tahir

It is said that he was one of the sons of Imam Zainul Abedeen A.S.

Raudhah of Sheikh Sudduque

He was a great A'alem and was born by the dua of our 12th Imam A.S.

Koahe Bibi Shahrbanoo A.S.

She was the wife of Imam Husayn A.S. and the mother of Ali Asghar. It is narrated that Imam Husayn A.S. instructed Bibi Shahrbanoo that after he is martyred in Karbala' she should mount the white horse "Zuljana" who will take her back to Iran.

She followed the instructions and truly "Zuljana" took her took her to Iran but her brothers in Iran did not accept her since she married an Arab so she was very sad. She went to live on the mountains of Shimran and it is believed that she entered one of the caves and never returned.

People come here with their Haajat and are fulfilled.

Museum of Teheran

Formerly this was the palace of Shah Reza and if you get a chance and time you should visit it.

Teheran/Mashad

You must make sure that you have a confirmed ticket Teheran/Mashad/Teheran otherwise it will be difficult to get a seat on the flight.

Mashad

Raudhah of Imam Ali Ridha' A.S.

He was born in Medina on Thursday 11th Zilkaad in the year 148 A.H. He was the son of our 7th Imam – Imam

Musa al-Kadhim A.S. and his mother's name was Ummul Banin Najma. Upon the death of his father, he became Imam, at the age of 35 years. Imam Ridha' A.S. lived in Medina, but Mamoon invited him to Mashad also known as Khorasan. Mamoon's main aim was to subdue the troubled Persian Province and he realized that Imam Ridha' A.S. was the only person who can achieve peace in Iran formerly known as Persia.

The Imam was reluctant to leave Medina, where he was leading a quite life, but under the circumstances, he had no choice, so he came to Khorasan. On arrival, Mamoon gave the Imam a royal reception and treated him with honour and declared his intention of making the Imam his successor.

Imam Ridha' A.S. told Mamoon openly "I know why you are doing this but there is no point in refusing because my death will come before yours." Mamoon forced the Imam and thus on 27th Ramadhan in the year 201 A.H., Imam Ridha' A.S. was officially designated as Mammon's heir. A gold coin was minted in the name of the Imam A.S. Distribution of this coin amongst the people subdued the enemies of the emporia and Mamoon's purpose was accomplished. Within 18 months, Persia was under control. Later Mamoon poisoned the Imam by feeding him with poisoned grapes, and made a great show of his sorrow. Thus our 8th Imam – Imam Ali Ridha' A.S. died on 17th Safar 203 A.H. at the age of 55 years and is buried here.

Our Imam is also well known as "Imam Dhamin" and this is due to a famous story narrated by historian that one day was travelling he saw a hunter capture a deer and wanted to slay it but he saw that the dear was crying and had tears in her eyes. The deer addressed our Imam in her language, and told him that she had babies who needed to be fed by her and that he should request the hunter to let her go and feed her babies first. The Imam fully understood the language of the dear and told the hunter to let the deer go and that after she fed her babies she would return to the hunter. The hunter was not prepared to listen to this and told the Imam if he will guaranty the return of the mother deer then, he will let her go. The Imam guaranteed and that is why he is known as Imam Dhamin.

If you visit the huge lecture room which was been built after the birth of the Islamic Republic of Iran you will see the artist has beautiful drawn the story of the deer on one of the walls.

Goharshad Masjid

It is said that Goharshad Khatoon, wife of an Indian King whose name was Shah Rukh Mirza, built this Masjid.

Museum of Quraan in The Haram of The Raudhah of Imam Ridha' A.S.

One should not miss the opportunity to visit this museum. It has pages of the Quraan written by hand by Imam Ali A.S., Imam Zainul Abedeen A.S. and other Imams.

Lunch as a Guest of Imam Ridha' A.S.

You may not get this opportunity again. You should take your passport and go to the office of Pilgrims which is situated in the Haram of Imam Ridha"s A.S. They will mark your passport and give you a ticket for the meal. At this restaurant they feed 4000 Zuwar each day. Thousands of Iranians have to wait for years before they get a chance to have a meal at this restaurant.

They serve you a good portion of rice and chicken and one cannot finish it, besides at the entrance you will find thousands of Iranian begging you to bring them some food (Niaz) from the Restaurant. We suggested you take with you a few zip lock bags and put the food in it and when you come out you can distribute them to the people waiting for this once in a lifetime "Tabaruk" but you must be very careful because they will jump on you like bees jump on the beehive.

There are many Ziyarat around Mashad and you should try and visit them all.

Tomb of Imamzada Sultan Ahmed R.A.

Tomb of Khwaja Abu Salt Harvi R.A.

He was a good friend of Imam Ridha' A.S. When the Imam was poisoned by Mamoon and lay on his dying bed, Imam said his last Vasiyat (Will) to Abu Salt.

Tomb of Khwaja Rabi R.A.

He too was the friend of Imam Ridha' A.S. He narrated many incidences on the life of the Imam and has also written many books.

Tomb of Khwaja Murad R.A.

Museum of Ferdowsi

He was a great poet.

Qadamghah

It is believed that Imam Ridha' A.S., while on his way to Tous in the 9th century made a stop here and delivered his speech to the audience who had gathered to welcome him to Neishapur. It is narrated that he said his Salaat on a slab of stone and left his footprints on the slab, which is now mounted on the wall.

There is also a spring water coming out from the rocks and is said to be a Miracle of our Imam where people drink the water in a special bowl for Shafa.

Tomb of Attr

He was a poet.

Tomb of Kamal-Al-Mulk

He was also a great artist.

Tomb of Omar Khayyam

He was an astronomical mathematician and a famous poet. His work is well known in the Muslim world.

Raudhah of Sayyed Ibrahim A.S.

He was the brother of Imam Ridha' A.S. and was also executed by the Bani Abbsi representative

Tour of Neishapur City

Shiraz – Shah Shiragh A.S.

The Raudhah of Shah Shiragh A.S. the brother of Imam Ridha' A.S. is in Shiraz. If you plan to visit then you have to add 2 to 3 extra days in your itinerary.

Your Ziyarat of iran is now almost complete and you have two choices either return to Damascus or proceed to Iraq. We recommend you go to Iraq from Amman, Jordan

Teheran/Damascus/Amman

Your flight by Air Iran is late in the evening and you will arrive Damascus sometime 8:00 PM. Usually all Raudhah in Damascus are closed after Isha Salaat. If you arrive on a Thursday night you may be lucky if your flight is not delayed then you proceed to Raudhah of Bibi Zainab A.S. direct from the airport before you go to your hotel.

Our experience tells us that it is better to go to Iraq from Amman, Jordan, because there is a good traffic on this road. You can also go from Iran but there you have change the buses at the border and you may have to walk about a half km to the Iraqi border and get your Immigration and customs cleared there.

They are talking of opening the road from Damascus but up to now it has not materialised. Of course the traveling time may be reduced by about 3 to 4 hours on this route.

Another reason to go from Amman is that you can visit Baitul-Muqaddas and other Ziyarat both in and around Amman and in and around Baitul-Muqaddas.

Amman - Jordan

Information for Jordanian Visa

They are very strict especially Zuwars holding Tanzanian, Kenyan, Ugandan, Indian, Pakistani and Shri Lankan passports.

You must obtain your Visa from the country of your residence before you proceed to Syria. If you are going to go to Baitul-Muqaddas and or Iraq then please make sure that you have multiple visas for Jordan otherwise you will have difficulties returning from Baitul-Muqaddas or Iraq.

Canadians and Americans can obtain their visa at the Amman airport, but we still recommend you obtain it from Canada and the United States before you travel to Jordan.

If you have joined a group, the organizer (of your group) will be responsible for obtaining your visa.

Hotels & Restaurants

In addition to five star Hotels mentioned in this booklet, there are also many 2 and 3 star hotels at the city centre, which are affordable.

Traveller's Cheques

Traveler's cheques can be easily cashed at shops and hotels.

Credit Cards

All major credit cards are acceptable in all shops and hotels in Jordan.

Currencies

There is no exchange control in Jordan but their money, which is known as JD, is expensive. In December 1997 one JD was equal to 2.5 American Dollars.

Weather

During the months of December, January, February and March are very cold and you will require thermal undergarments, a winter coat and winter gloves.

March, April, August, September and October and are pleasant months.

June and July are very hot.

There are beautiful Mosques and historical buildings in Amman, which is worth visiting.

• **Tomb of Ja'far at-Tayyar**

• **The Seven Sleepers**

• **The Dead Sea**

• **Prophet Shoab A.S.**

Amman/Baitul-Muqaddas

It is about a one and half-hour drive from Amman to the Jerusalem border. It is advisable to proceed early in the morning after breakfast.

Information for Jordanian Visa

They are very strict especially with those visitors holding a Tanzanian, Kenyan, Ugandan, Indian, Pakistani or a Shri Lankan passport. You must obtain your visa from the country of residence before you proceed to Baitul-Muqaddas. You must make sure that they do not stamp your passport with the Israeli Visa or else you will not be able to enter any Arab country except Jordan. Usually we get them to give us Visa on a piece of paper.

Canadians and Americans can obtain their visa at the Israel border, but we still recommend that you make arrangements with any Tour Operator in Amman to obtain for you the Israeli Visa on a piece of paper.

If you have joined a group then the organizer of your group will be responsible for obtaining your Visa.

Hotels & Restaurants

There are many five star hotels in the Jewish area of Jerusalem but Muslim Tour Operators in Amman are very reluctant to accommodate Muslims at these hotels. They will accommodate Muslims in 3 or 4 star hotels in the Muslim section of Jerusalem.

Traveller's Cheques

Traveler's cheques can be easily cashed at shops and hotels.

Credit Cards

All major credit cards are acceptable in all shops and hotels in Jordan.

Weather

During the months of December, January, February and March are very cold and you may require thermal undergarments, winter coat and winter gloves.

March, April, August, September and October and are pleasant months. June and July are very hot.

If you intend to go to Bait-ul-Muqaddas then make sure you make arrangements with a Tour Operator before your arrival in Amman otherwise it may day you days before you can obtain a visa from Amman. Usually the Tour Operator makes arrangements to drive you to the Israeli border where you have to clear Immigration and Customs. There are no problems with Canadian and American Passport holders. Others Nationalities could be a problem.

Please make sure you tell your Tour Operator that the Israeli Visa should not be stamped in your passport otherwise you will not be able to visit any Arab Countries.

The Tour Operator who will be responsible looking after you in Israel will come and pick you up at the border and drive you to Bait-ul-Muqaddas.

Bait-ul-Muqaddas

This was our first Qibla before it was changed to Khan al-Ka'aba in Makkah. The event took place at Masjid al-Qiblatain in Medina.

Masjid al-Aqsa

Tomb of Nabi Musa A.S.

Bethlehm City Where Nabi Isa A.S. Was Born

There are many Christians and Muslims historical monuments. If time permits, visit the Diamond Factory.

Al-Quds/Amman

After you return to Amman from Al-Quds first you should try to rest for a night and prepare yourself for the long bus journey to Iraq.

If you are going for Ziyarat to Iraq then please continue reading

Ziyarat of Iraq

Please refer to page numbers 10 to 14, which are very important except for a few changes for Ziyarat in Iraq, which are mentioned below.

Information for Iraq Visa

You must obtain your Visa from the country of your residence before you proceed to Iraq. If you are going to go to Iraq from Amman, Jordan, then please make sure that you have multiple visas for Jordan otherwise you will have problem when you return from Iraq.

At the Iraqi border you will have to take an Aid test and you will have to pay US$50 cash for it. Some groups include this in their cost.

We highly recommend that you join a group for going to Iraq for Ziyarat.

The United States has a Presidential decree that no American citizen is permitted to go into Iraq, if they do so and the government comes to learn of it they may be denied entry into the United States. Therefore, Zuwars are cautioned that the groups they are joining do not get the Iraqi visa stamped in the passport; it should be obtained on a piece of paper, which does not present a problem.

Even the Canadian Government will not be able to help Canadians if they get stuck in Iraq. So it is important to join a respectable and well-known group.

Items to Take With on Your Iraq Trip

List of items

01) One bottle of Shampoo and soap.
02) One can dusting powder.
03) One toothbrush and toothpaste.
04) One hairbrush or comb.
05) One travelling money pouch for safe keeping your valuables.
06) Four shirts, two pants, two pajamas and some undergarments for men.
07) Four sets of Shalwaar Kurta or long dress and some undergarments for women.
08) One Janamaaz (Mussalla).
09) One travelling alarm clock.
10) One pair of rubber slippers and one pair of **very comfortable shoes for daily wear.**
11) You should take enough prescription medicine to last you during the entire trip and you should carry them in your hand luggage. Also please make sure to take some **Tylenol** and cough drops like **'Bradasol' for sore throat.**

12) A First Aid Kit.

13) If you wear prescription glasses then it is highly recommended to carry (with you) an extra pair.
14) Packages of soup, dry snacks, tea, coffee, coffee mate, cookies, chevda, Ghanthia, chewing gum, candies, and chocolates etc. To buy these from Iraq is difficult.
15) There is a lot of poverty in Iraq so if you can then take some clothes and medicine to give them

away to the needy. You might want also to take some candies and chocolates for the children near the Haram.

Hotels

The quality of hotels in Iraq is not very high standard. Most of the Hotels in Karbala' and Najaf are poorly equipped and do not have English style bathrooms in all the rooms, so if you are disabled please make sure you carry (with you) a portable toilet.

Currencies

There is exchange control in Iraq and Zuwars are advised not to cash their currency in stores but to ask their group organizer to exchange their money for them through the Tour Operator. We recommend you carry US Dollars bills (with you) in a mix denomination. Have some dollar bills to give away as 'Baqshees".

The exchange rate varies from month to month. You will not be able to reconvert the Iraqi Dinar to US Dollars. Last December 1997 the rate was about 1600 Iraqi Dinar to one US Dollar.

Weather

During the months of December, January, February and March are very cold and you will require thermal undergarments, winter coat and winter gloves.

March, April, September and October are pleasant months.

May, June, July and August are very hot months.

Amman/Najaf

Najaf is about 53 miles from Karbala'. It has been narrated that there was a huge mountain where the city of Najaf is now. When Prophet Nooh A.S. son refused to
get in the ark, he got on that mountain thinking it would save him from drowning.

Prophet Nooh A.S. prayed to the Almighty Allah to save his son but Allah's reply was that he could not accept his prayers as his son had disobeyed Allah's instructions to get into the ship.

The mountain suddenly fell to pieces and an ocean gushed out. This ocean was called NAY. After several years the ocean dried up and the place was then called NAY-JAFF (Dry Ocean). Later it came to be known as NAJAF.

It is also the city of Madressas for Ulemas and many renowned Ulemas like Ayatullah Burujardi, Ayatullah Mohsin Hakim, The Grand Ayatullah Abul Qassim El Khoue are buried in and around the Holy Haram of Imam Ali A.S.

Hazrat Imam Ali A.S.

He was the son of Hazrat Abu Talib and Bibi Fatima Binte Asad. The Prophet of Islam (SAW) raised him. He was always protecting the Holy Prophet during his Prophetic Mission.

He was married to the only daughter of the Prophet of Allah (SAW), Bibi Fatima Zehra A.S. and he was the proud father of Imam Hassan A.S., Imam Husayn A.S., Bibi Zainab A.S. and Hazrat Abbas A.S.

He was the hero of many the battle of Islam. It is narrated that the Prophet on many occasion said that "Ali is never separated from the truth and the truth is never separated from him"

At Ghadeer the Prophet proclaimed Imam Ali A.S. to be his brother and the leader of Muslims after him, but the people of the time ignored this and chose another leader whilst Imam Ali A.S. was busy with the burial rituals for the Prophet.

When the third elected leader was killed the people of the time begged Imam Ali A.S. to be the ruler. He accepted and ruled with justice and truth in the Islamic way.

On the 19th of Ramadhan, in the Masjid of Kufa, (while he was praying Fajr Salaat), he was struck by Abdul Rehman Ibne Muljim (may the curse of Allah fall upon him) with a sword. He died two days later and is buried in Najaf where Inshallah you will visit to pay your respect.

Prophet Adam A.S.

The first Prophet of Allah, was Prophet Adam A.S. who was created from clay by the spirit of Allah (SWT).

As soon as he was created, all the angels were ordered to prostrate to him. All obeyed except Shaitaan. Shaitaan was then ordered to leave Heaven, which he did. However, requested Allah to allow him to live as long as human beings live on the earth. His wish was granted.

One day Shaitaan came and fooled Prophet Adam A.S. and Bibi Hawwa A.S. to eat a fig from a tree. They ate the fig, which Allah (SWT) had ordered them not to touch. go near that tree. Immediately they realised their mistake and asked Allah (SWT) to forgive them. They were forgiven but were asked to leave Jannat and live on the earth.

Hazrat Adam is buried next to Prophet Nooh A.S. and Imam Ali A.S. is buried next to Prophet Nooh A.S.

Prophet Nooh A.S.

The people were giving Prophet Nooh A.S. a very hard time and were not prepared to accept that they should believe in one God. So, Allah (SWT) asked him to build an ark (ship) on which only the believing people could board with various kind of animal. The disbeliivers including one of his sons refused to board the Ark stayed behind on the mountain. The mountain crushed and all the bad people who took refuge on it were drowned.

Allama Hilli A.R.

He derived the name 'Hilli' from the village in the out -skirt of Najaf where he was born. He became a Mujtahid before he was baligh. He was one of the greatest "Uremia" and he died in Hilla. He is buried in the "Sahan" of Imam Ali's A.S. Raudhah.

Muqaddas Ardebilli A.R.

t is narrated that he once went to get water to perform wudhoo from a well. Instead of the water a he treasure came out. He put them back saying that he wanted water for wudhoo not treasures. He is buried in Najaf and his real name is Mullah Ahmed bin Mohamed. He too is just buried in the

'Sahan' of Imam Ali A.S. Raudhah.

Makam al-Imam Zainul Abedeein A.S.

This is the place where Imam Zainul Abedeen A.S. used to spend hours in prayers. He like this place because if faces the Raudhah of Imam Ali A.S. Zuwar visit this place and recite munajats.

Prophet Hood A.S.

The people of his time were very rich and due to their wealth they were very strong and worshipped idols.

Prophet Hood A.S. repeatedly warned them to give up worshipping the idols and to turn towards one God but they did not listen. Allah (SWT) punished them and they were all killed except Prophet Hood A.S. and a few believers. His tomb is at Wadius Salaam, in Najaf.

Prophet Saleh A.S.

Allah (SWT) sent Prophet Saleh A.S. to Thamood. Allah sent a she-camel and instructed Prophet Saleh A.S. to tell the people of Thamood that they should not kill it. They did not listen and killed the she-camel. Allah (SWT) punished them by sending an earthquake and fire and they were all destroyed. His tomb is at Wadius Salaam.

Some 400 km from Medina in Saudi Arabia there is a city known as "Madain Saleh". Many foreigners go to visit the ruins of this city. Allah (SWT) brought his curse on this city and the people there in.

Makam al-Saheb-Ul Asr A.S.

It is narrated that Saheb-ul Asr visits this place which is in the boundaries of Wadius Salaam.

Makam al-Imam Ja'far Sadiq A.S.

This is also in the boundaries of Wadius Salaam.

Tomb Hazrat Kumail A.R.

He was one of the favorite companion of Imam Ali A.S. IMAM ALI A.S taught the famous dua Kumail that is recited on every Thursday to him.

Tomb of Hazrat Rashid Hijri A.R.

He was the companion of Imam Ali A.S. who had come from Yemen to Kufa. He was one of the most important friend of our Imam. One day Imam Ali A.S. asked him "what will you do if Bani Ummayah asks you to leave me?"

Rashid Al Hijri in turn asked our Imam "that if I do not leave you what will be my fate?" The Imam, replied "in that case you will be with me in Jannat", to which Rashid Al Hijri replied, "so I will not leave you."

It is narrated that after the Shahadat of our Imam, Abidalla Ben Ziad sent for Rashid Al Hijri and sked him to curse Imam Ali A.S. and his sons. When he refused to do so his hands and feet were ut off. Rashid Hijri continued to praise Imam Ali A.S. and Abidalla asked him to stop, but he would not, so his tongue was cut off.

Masjid al-Hannaana

This Masjid is between Kufa and Najaf. The fazilat of this Masjid is that when Hazrat Imam Hassan A.S. and Hazrat Imam Husayn A.S. together with others carried the 'Janaza' of Hazrat Imam Ali A.S. from Kufa to Najaf they passed near this Masjid. At that time the pillars of this Masjid inclined for ta'azim."

It is narrated that Hannan use to be a Church. When IMAM HUSAYN A.S. was martyred on the 10th of Muharram, Bani Ummayah carried his head on a plate. When Bani Ummayah passed by this hurch, now Masjid, the priest noticed that the face of Imam Husayn A.S. was shinning with light (noor) was coming out and was reciting an Ayah from the Holy Quran. So, the priest asked Bani Ummayah to leave the head with him for one night and e addressed the head "who are you?" and the head replied I am Husayn Bin Ali and my grandfather is Prophet Muhammad (SAW) and Bani Ummayah in Karbala' killed me. The priest was moved with the reply and he immediately accepted Islam.

Ziyarats in Hilla

Hazrat Hamza A.S.

One of Hazrat Abbas A.S. son's whose name was Ubaydullah was a resident of Medina. He was a great scholar of his time and he left a son named Hassan who also was a great scholar and Hazrat Hamza A.S. happens to be one of his sons. So he is the great grandson of Hazrat Abbas A.S.

Raudhah Of Muhammad Bine Imam Ali A.S.

He is also known as Baqar.

Raudhah Of Prophet Hazrat Ayub A.S.

Masjid Marad-Us-Shams

is narrated that Imam Ali A.S. was nursing one of his sick son and the time of Asr passed and started entering into Maghrib. The Imam was very sad and looked at the sun. Through the mercy of Allah (SWT) the sun reverted to Asr time and the Imam said his Asr Salaat.

Raudhah Of Janab al-Qasim Bin Imam Moosa al-Kadhim A.S.

He is the brother of Imam Ridha' A.S. who was heard saying that if you cannot visit me in Mashad then you should visit my brother in Iraq.

Karbala' – There Are Many Ziyarats

Karbala' al-Moa'lla, started as a small village to grow into a famous city in Iraq and is known worldwide since the martyrdom of Hazrat Imam Husayn A.S. It is situated six miles from Baghdad. In the centre of the city is the sacred Raudhah of Hazrat Imam Husayn A.S. Within a walking distance one may visit the sacred Raudhah of Hazrat Qamar al-Bani Hashim, Hazrat Abul Fadhilil

Abbas A.S. The dome and minarets of Imam Husayn's Raudhah are covered with gold. It is the same field on which he was martyred on the 10th Muharram 61 AH under extremely cruel circumstances with his family and friends after suffering three days of thirst and hunger.

This great sacrifice ensured the survival of Islam as long as the world exists. It is highly recommended (Makhsusi) to be in Karbala' on a Thursday Night for the Ziyarat of Imam Husayn A.S., and his companions.

Under the Dome and just touching the Zaree of our Imam is a piece of red coloured stone where we are told that we should recite two rakaat Salaat and ask for our Haajat which Inshallah will be fulfilled.

There are only four places where you can recite full Salaat even though the condition of ten days is not met. They are in Medina, Makkah, Raudhah of Imam Husayn A.S. under the Dome and Masjid al-Kufa.

Hazrat Ali Akbar A.S.

He was Imam Husayn's A.S. eldest son. He was 18 years old when he gave his life for Islam on the fields of Karbala'. It is narrated that whenever Imam Husayn A.S. wanted to do Ziyarat of the Prophet of Allah, he would look at Hazrat Ali Akbar A.S. because of his resemblance to the Holy Prophet.

On the morning of Ashura at the time of Fajr Salaat, Imam Husayn A.S. asked Ali Akbar A.S. to recite Adhaan.

He is buried next to Imam Husayn A.S.

Ali Asghar A.S.

He was the youngest son of Imam Husayn A.S. who was only 6 months old. He is also known as Abdullah Tiflan al-Ardhia). When all the relatives and the companions were martyred, Imam Husayn A.S. went to fetch Ali Asgher A.S. and told him something in his ears. Immediately the baby jumped into the Imam's arms.

The Imam covered him with his Aba and took him towards the army of Yazid. Yazid thought that the Imam had brought the Holy Quran and was going to ask for mercy, but instead the Imam put the baby on the hot sand of Karbala' and spoke to the army loudly and told them that if he (the Imam) was at fault then the 6 months old baby was not and that they should come and give the baby some water.

They did not but instead Hurmala (may curse of Allah on him) pulled a three headed arrow and aimed at the baby piercing his little neck and the arm of Imam Husayn A.S.

He too is buried next to our Imam.

Ganj al-Shohada

This is a mass grave where all the Shohad al-Karbala' are buried. It is narrated that even Shah Qassim the son of Imam Hassan A.S. is buried in here.

Qatlagha

This is the place where Shimr Maloon (may the curse of Allah be upon him) sat on Imam Husayn's A.S. chest and martyred him..

Hazrat Habib Ibne Mazahir A.S.

He was the childhood friend of Imam Husayn A.S. When he reached Karbala' and so that the army of Yazid surrounded him he sent a letter to Habib informing him of the situation and asking him to come to Karbala' to help the Imam. Immediately, Habib came to Karbala' and went to fight for Islam and was martyred on the day of Ashura.

His tomb is just outside one of the doors to the Raudhah of Imam Husayn A.S.

Hazrat Ibraheem Bin Musa Kadhim A.S.

At one time he was the governor of Yemen. He was the grandfather of Sayyid Murtaza A.R. and too was martyred by the Abbaside Caliph.

His tomb is just outside the Raudhah of Imam Husayn A.S.

Till al-Zainabia

This is a small hill facing the Raudhah of Imam Husayn A.S. and it is from this hill that she was witnessing the fight of her beloved brother Imam Husayn A.S., his family and companions.

Khaimagah

This is just behind Tille-Zainabia. Here all the tents of Imam Husayn A.S., his family and companions were pitched.

Raudhah Of Hazrat Abbas A.S.

He was the stepbrother of Imam Husayn A.S. and his mother's name is Ummul-Banin. When Imam Ali A.S. was on his death bed he called Hazrat Abbas A.S. and put his hands in the hands of Imam Husayn A.S. and told Hazrat Abbas that this, pointing to Imam Husayn A.S. is your master and that you are like his slave so on in Karbala' on the day of Ashura you must help him and fight for Islam until death. Hazrat Abbas A.S. just proved that on the day of Ashura.

It is said that the distance between the Raudhah of Imam Husayn A.S. and Hazrat Abbas A.S. is the same as the distance between Safa and Marwa in Makkah.

Under the Raudhah of Hazrat Abbas A.S. there is a river running and is called Al-Kamma, though they have closed the entrance and is opened only to high dignitaries coming to Iraq from other countries.

It is narrated that a King by the name of Al-Kamma had stopped at Karbala' and was very sad. So he tried to find out what this place was and why it looked very sad to him. The people told him that this place is called Karbala' and one of the son's of Prophet Muhammad (SWT) and his family will be martyred here on the day of Ashura and they will be denied water of the river Euphrates which we call 'Furat"

The king felt sorry and ordered that a canal be dug from the river Euphrates to the place where now stands the Raudhah of Hazrat Abbas A.S. unfortunately this did not help Imam Husayn A.S. on the day of Ashura.

Kafl Abbas

Kafl Abbas means the arm of Hazrat Abbas A.S. There were two spots near by outside the Haram of Hazrat Abbas A.S. One was destroyed during the Persian Gulf war and the second one is still there.

Hazrat Hurr

He was the commander of one of the Yazid's battalion and he was sent by Yazid to stop Imam Husayn A.S., his family and companions from going to Kufa unless and until Imam Husayn A.S. gives 'Bayat" (allegiance) to Yazid. When he arrived at the Imam's camp, he (Hurr) and his entire battalion including horses were dying of thirst. Immediately Imam Husayn A.S. gave orders to Hazrat Abbas A.S. that they be given water until their thirst including the horses are quenched, though the were the enemies of the Imam.

On the night of Ashura Hurr could not sleep after hearing the cries of small children from Imam Husayn's camps crying for water. Early in the morning he asked his servant to tie his hands behind his backs and he went straight to Imam's camp. When he was near the came he came down his horse and walked to where the Imam was and fell on his knees asking for forgiveness. Imam raised him up and told him that Allah (SWT) has forgiven you.

Hurr asked permission from the Imam to go and fight for Islam which he did but after sometime he was martyred and he is buried about 3 miles away from the city of Karbala'.

Raudhah of Janab al-Aun A.S.

He was the son of Bibi Zainab A.S. and he too was killed on the day of Ashura. He is buried some 10 miles from the city of Karbala'.

Raudhah of Mohamed & Ibrahim

They were the two sons of Hazrat Muslim Bin Aqeel A.S. and they were going to Imam Husayn A.S. to give him the message that their father had been killed. They were caught by Haris (may Allah send His curse upon him).

They are buried about 25 miles from the city of Karbala' in the Musayyab area.

Ziyarat in Madayan

Mazaar of Salman al-Farsi A.R.

His original name of Rozeba and he was an Iranian from Iran formerly known as Persia. The Prophet of Allah (SAW) changed his name to Salman.

IMAM ALI A.S. made him a governor of Madayan but he died at the age of 88 years, a few weeks after his arrival in Madayan.

Mazaar Huzaifa al-Yemani A.R.

He was one of the companions of our Prophet and it is narrated that when he used to recite Munajats, the Angels used to come from heaven to listen to him.

Mazaar of Jabir Bin Abdallah Ansari A.R.

He was also one of the close companion of the Holy Prophet. It is narrated that the Holy Prophet told him that we would see the 5th Imam, Muhammad Baqir A.S., and to give his is salaams.

It is said that when he came to Karbala', he first went to Nehr al-Furat, did Ghusl wore Ihram and then visited the graves of the Shohada al-Karbala'.

In the year 1934, Nuripasha the Vazir (Vice-President) of Shah Faisal the king of Iraq at that time, so a dream for three continuous days whereby Jabir told him that water was coming into his grave and that of Huziafa's. He asked him to transfer them to another grave.

Nuripasha narrated the dream to Shah Faisal who said that he also had the same dream.

It was decided to transfer the bodies to another grave, which was announced. On 26th March 1934 and it was announced in the PTI News Agency worldwide. Some Germans reports also came to witness the transfer of the bodies. When the bodies were taken out of the graves they were intact with the same Kafan. Even the eyes were wide open with so much 'noor' and the hair of beard was still wet as if the bodies had just been given Ghusl. t. Salaat al-Mayyat was prayed again. The army saluted and the bodies were transferred to another gravesite next to Hazrat Salaman al-Farsi A.R. Many Germans reporters when witnessing this accepted Islam.

Tak al-Kisra

This used to be the summer palace of the King of Persia whose name was Nausherwaan. Because t can get very cold in Iran during winter. He built this some 1700 years ago and used to come and stay there during the severe winter months.

It is narrated that when the Prophet of Allah (SAW) was born, the famous arch in it, which is known as the Arch of, Catesiphon, developed cracks in it. Visitors can still see the arch as well as the cracks in it.

Masjid al-Kufa

It is narrated that many Prophets have visited this Masjid and have performed Salaat, that is why there are many places where Zuwar recite Ziyarat and perform two rakaat Salaat. You will find the sketch of the Masjid on page number 139.

1. Main Entrance

2. Makam al-Hazrat Ibrahim a.s.
This is the same Prophet that built the Ka'aba in Makkah and was ready to sacrifice his son Hazrat Ismaeel at Munna.

3. Makam al-Hazrat Khizr A.S.
He is still arrive and one of his miracles is that when leans on a dry stick it becomes fresh green.

4. Place of Miracle
It is narrated that during the time Imam Ali A.S. a group of people wanted to stone a woman to

death because they thought that she had committed adultery as her stomach was bulging just like that of a pregnant woman.

Imam Ali A.S. had happened to be present at this place and he was asked to give his decision. Imam Ali A.S. asked them to bring a big tub and told them to fill it with water and put a curtain round it. Then she asked the woman to go and sit in this tube, which she did and after some time her stomach returned to her normal shape and it was proved that she was not pregnant.

5. Court of Imam Ali A.S.
This is the place where Imam Ali A.S. used conduct his daily court.

6. Well of Hazrat Nooh A.S.
Hazrat Nooh A.S. had also visited Masjid al-Kufa. In fact inside the Masjid there is a place where the arc of Nabi Nooh stood.

7. Entrance to the Well

This used to be the entrance to the well of Hazrat Nooh A.S.

8. Makam al-Hazrat Muhammad A.S.
This is the place where the Prophet of Islam used to stay and pray when visiting visit Masjid al-Kufa.

9. Makam al-Hazrat Adam A.S.
This is the place where Hazrat Adam A.S. used to stay and pray when visiting Masjid al-Kufa.

10. Makam al-Jibra'el A.S.
This is the place where Hazrat Jibra'el A.S. used to stay and pray when visiting Masjid al-Kufa.

11. Makam al-Imam Ja'far Sadiq A.S.
This is the place where Hazrat Imam Ja'far Sadiq A.S. used to stay and pray when visiting Masjid al-Kufa.

12. Makam al-Zainul Abedeen A.S.
This is the place where Hazrat Imam Zainul Abdedeen A.S. used to stay and pray when visiting Masjid al-Kufa.

13. Makam al-Hazrat Nooh A.S.
This is the place inside Masjid al-Kufa where the ark of Hazrat Nooh A.S. stood.

14. Shahadat Place of Imam Ali A.S.
Inside Masjid al-Kufa our Imam was struck by a poisoned sword by Ibn al-Muljeem on the 19th day of Ramadhan.

15. Place Where Imam Ali A.S. Used To Pray During The Night

16. Ruaza of Hazrat Muslim-Ibne-Aqil A.S.
Just outside the boundary of Masjid al-Kufa is the Raudhah of Hazrat Muslim Ibne Aqil A.S. He was the cousin of Imam Husayn A.S. who had sent him to Kufa as his deputy before him but was killed by Yazid's men.

17. Mazaar of Mukhtar A.R.
He was the first person to took the revenge of Imam Husayn A.S.

18. Mazaar of Hazrat Hani Ibne Urwa A.R.
Hazrat Muslim A.S. stayed at Hani's House when he arrived in Kufa. Hani too was then killed by Yazid's men.

Raudhah Of Khadijatul Kubra Binte Imam Ali A.S.

Just outside Masjid al-Kufa and across the road is the Raudhah of Khadijatul Kubra.

House of Imam Ali A.S.

Behind Masjid al-Kufa is the house of our Imam and inside the house there is a place where Imam Ali A.S. lay on his deathbed in the presence of his family members.

There is also a room where it is said that Imam Ali A.S. was given Ghusl at the place.

Further up there is a well and Zuwar take the water for Tabaruk. It is better to put on your arms and forehead and just touch the tongue for Shafa.

Matham Bin Tammar A.R.

He was a close companion of Imam Ali A.S. and also was his business partner running a date shop. The name Tammar is derived from Tamr that means dates. He too was killed for his love of Imam Ali A.S.

It is narrated that a wealth businessman came to Najaf from Karachi with his son who had blood cancer. He visited Imam Ali's A.S. Raudhah in Najaf he cried, prayed and made a wish that if his son is cured then he will get any kind of work to be done at the Imam's Raudhah. With the blessings of Allah (SWT) and the dua of Imam Ali A.S. his son recovered completely and as he had made a wish he went back to Najaf and asked the Mutavallis if there is any work that has to be done or completed at the Imam.s Raudhah.

The Mutavallis replied that off hand they do not know but they will think about it. At night when the Mutavalli was sleeping he dreamed that Imam Ali told him that do not do any work in my Raudhah, but instead, build the Raudhah of Maytham's properly because it is in very bad shape. So the work was done on Maytham's Raudhah.

Raudhah of Zaid Bin Ali Bin Alhussain Bin Imam Ali A.S.

SKETCH OF MASJID-E-SAHLAH.

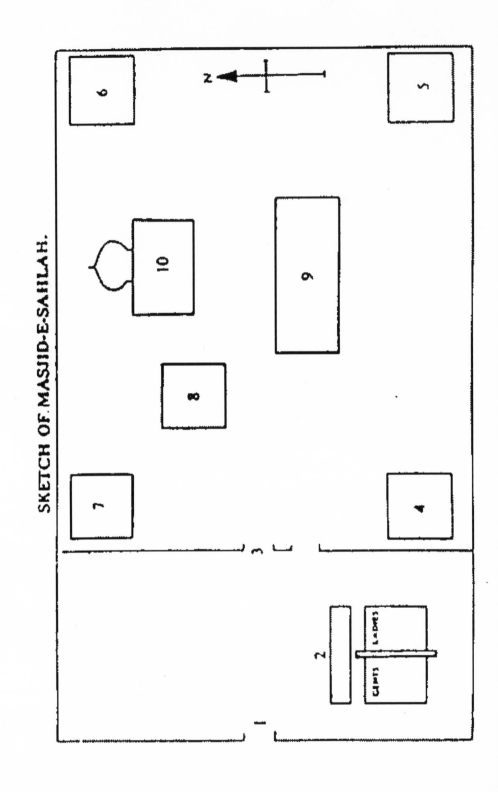

Al Hajjaj asked Zaid Bin Ali to curse Imam Ali A.S. otherwise he will be killed. He refused, so he was killed and his body was hung on the palm tree for four years till he was dried and the palm tree started growing branches besides the main trunk of the tree, which is unusual, but it grew and is still there until this day. We have been told there is no such kind of a tree anywhere in Iraq. If the palm tree with all it's extension is cut it at the top, it will be noticed that it forms a letter 'Allah" in Arabic. This can be witnessed in one of our Ziyarat videocassette.

Sketch of Masjid al-Kufa

1. - Main entrance 10. - Makam al-Jibra'el A.S.

2. - Makam al-Hazrat Ibrahim A.S. 11. - Makam al-Imam Ja'far Sadiq A.S.

3. - Makam al-Hazrat Khizer A.S. 12. - Makam al-Imam Zainul Abedeen A.S.

4. - Place of Miracle 13. - Makam al-Hazrat Nooh A.S..

5. - Court of Hazrat Imam Ali A.S. 14. - Shahadat Place of Imam Ali A.S.

6. - Well of Hazrat Nooh A.S. 15. - Night prayers place of Imam Ali A.S.

7. - Entrance to the well 16. - Raudhah of Hazrat Muslim Bin Aqil A.S..

8. - Makam al-Hazrat Muhammad A.S. 17. - Mazaar of Hazrat Mukhtar A.R.

9. - Makam al-Hazrat Adam A.S. 18. – Mazaar of Hazrat Hani Ibne Urwa A.R.

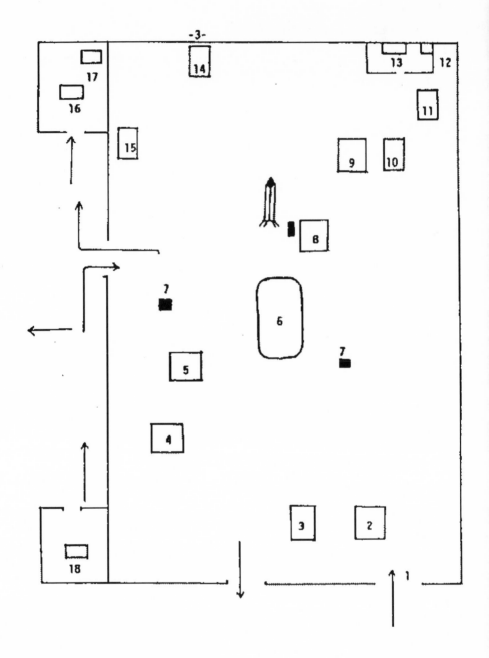

Sketch of Masjid al-Sahla

1. – General entrance 06, - Makam al-Hazrat Idris A.S.
2. – Place for Wadhu 07. - Makam al-Hazrat Khizer A.S.
3. – Main entrance 08. - Makam al-Imam Zainul Abedeen A.S.
4. – Makam al-Saleheen 09. - Makam al-Imam Ja'far Sadiq A.S.
5. – Makam al-Hazrat Ibrahim A.S. 10. - Makam al-Imam Hujjat A.S.

Masjid al-Sa'asa Ibne Sanhan A.R.

It is believed that here too the head of Imam Husayn A.S. was kept when Yazid was taking the heads of the Shoahada and the Bibi from Karbala' to Damascus via Kufa.

Masjid al-Sahla

It is the second most important Masjid after Kufa. It is also the house of Prophet Idrees A.S., Prophet Ibrahim A.S. and Prophet Khizer A.S.

At all places mentioned on page 140 Ziyarat is recited and two rakaat Salaat is prayed by all Zuwar.

1. General Entrance to the Masjid

2. Place for Doing Wadhoo

3. Main Entrance To The Masjid

4. Makam al-Saleheen
This is the general place for saying your prayers.

5. Makam al-Hazrat Ibrahim A.S.
This is the place where Hazrat Ibrahim A.S. used to visit and say his prayers.

6. Hazrat Makam al-Hazrat Idris A.S.
This is the place where Hazrat Ibrahim A.S. used to visit and say his prayers.

It is narrated that Imam Ja'far Al-Sadiq A.S. said that he had a vision and saw Imam Al Mahdi A.S. coming down in Al Sahla Masjid with his family and children and it is his place of residence.

It is also narrated that all the Prophets who were sent to this earth by Allah (SWT) had prayed in this Masjid and any Momineen who prays in this Masjid will come back to visit it again. There is also a rock there which has all the names of all the Prophets. It is also said that if one asks for Haajat here with a clean heart will Inshallah be fulfilled.

It is also believed that the Angles come to pray in this Masjid and also Imam Saheb-ul-Dhaman is always present in this Masjid for Ziyarat on Tuesday nights between Salaat al-Maghribain and Isha.

There are many Musallas where many Prophets and Imam have prayed and you can follow the sketch of Masjid al-Sahla given on page 142.

7. Makam al-Hazrat Khizer A.S.
This is the place where Hazrat Khizer A.S. used to visit and say his prayers.

8. Makam al-Zainul Abedeen A.S.
This is the place where Hazrat Imam Zainul Abedeen A.S. used to visit and say his prayers.

9. Makam al-Ja'far Sadiq A.S.
This is the place where Hazrat Imam Ja'far Sadiq A.S. used to visit and say his prayers.

10. Makam al-Imam Hujjat A.S.
This is the place where Hazrat Imam Hujjat A.S. visits and say his prayers. It is the practice of Zuwar to recited dua Tawasool at this place.

Samarrah

Samarrah used to be the capital of Iraq and is situated on the banks of river Tigris. The old city has, however, turned into ruins. The new city is located around the Raudhah that contains four tombs.

Raudhah of Imam Ali Naqi A.S.

He is our 10th Imam and he was the one that completed the rules of Taqlid to prepare believers for the occultation of 12th Imam.

Raudhah of Imam Hassan Askari A.S.

He is our 11th Imam and was kept under house arrest for a very long time. He was kept there because the ruler of the time did not want him to have a son, just like at the time of Hazrat Mussa A.S.

He was married to Bibi Nargis Khatun A.S. who gave birth to our 12th Imam. He became an Imam at the age of about four and half years when his father Imam Hassan Askari A.S. passed away. He led the Salaat al-Mayyat of his father.

Bibi Hakima Khatun A.S.

She taught Bibi Nargis Khatun A.S. about the rules of religion. She was present when the 12th Imam was born.

When our 11th Imam was put in jail, Bibi Hakima Khatun A.S. used to answer all the masaels, which the Shia Umah used to ask her. She was a very learned and pious lady.

Bibi Nargis Khatun A.S.

She was a princes from Roman who became a Muslim after seeing Bibi Fatima Zehra A.S. and the Holy Prophet (SAW) in her dream. She was the mother of our 12th Imam Mahdi A.S.

Our 11th Imam told Bibi Nargis Khatun A.S. that the army will enter our house to check whether any child is born to which Bibi Nargis Khatun A.S. told Imam, "Please pray for me that I die before they enter our house and make me their captive. She died before our 11th Imam's shahadat.

Imam Mahdi A.S. – Our 12th Imam

Our Imam has many titles like, Sahebul Asr - Lord of the period of time, Sahebuz Dhaman - Lord of the age, Mahdi - Guide.

He has the same name as our Holy Prophet that is Muhammad. He was born in Sammarrah and was under his father's care until his father was martyred. He became the Imam at the age of four and half years and went into occultation. He was only available to his deputies who were Uthman bin Saeed, Muhammad bin Uthman, then Husayn bin Rooh and finally Ali bin Muhammad Samarri. When the last of them was to die, Imam wrote to tell him that there would be more deputies after him and that he (Imam) was going into occultation until Allah (SWT) willed him to re-appear.

Makam al-Ghaibat of our 12th Imam A.S.

This is in the basement of the house of the 11th Imam A.S. where the shrine now stands. The entrance has been opened from the courtyard. It is said that this was the house of Bibi Nargis and our 12th Imam was last seen here.

Sayyid Muhammad Ibne Imam Ali Naqi A.S.

He was the son of Imam Ali Naqi A.S. the place where his Raudhah is used to be the cemetery of Shias. During the time of Hajjaj bin Yusuf thousands of shias were imprisoned here and when they died were buried there. No Shia was allowed to leave the area and because of the torment thousands of them died.

This Raudhah is very famous for couples who come to make a Nadr (wish) that they be blessed with a child. It is in Balad a small village near Samarrah.

Kadhmain

It is a twin city of Baghdad and just a bridge between them separates these two cities.

Raudhah of Imam Musa Kadhim A.S.

Zuwar usually enter through the gate which is known as 'Bab al-Murad' which means the gate of fulfillment of wishes.

He is our 7th Imam and he was given the title of Kadhim that means one who swallows his anger. He also has another title that is Baabul Hawaaj, which literally means the door of fulfillment of wishes.

Harun Rashid had imprisoned our Imam and then poisoned him and left his body on the bridge of Baghdad. His body stayed on the bridge for three days then his followers buried him.

If you are lucky to be present in Kadhmain on a Thursday night you will see that it is difficult to even touch the Zaree of the Imam.

Raudhah of Imam Muhammad Taqi A.S.

He is our 9th Imam and he became an Imam at the age of 9 years and even at this age he answered all questions of religion to all including the learned ones.

His Raudhah is next to the Raudhah of Imam Musa Kadhim A.S.

Tomb of Sheikh Mufeed A.R.

He was given title Mufeed means one who brings benefit. His real name is Muhammad bin Numan. Even our 12th Imam A.S. addressed him in the name of 'Mufeed'. It is said that he was the author of hundreds of books and one of the most important one being 'Kitabul'Irshaad' which is the life history of our 12 Imams.

His tomb is within the boundary of the Raudhah of our two Imams in Kadhemain and one can read the Marshia written

on his grave that was the same Marshia recited by our 12th Imam when 'Mufeed' died.

Tomb of Khwaja Nasiruddin Toosi A.R.

It is narrated that our 12th Imam A.S. taught Dua al-Tawassul in a dream to bin Muhammad bin Hasan that is his real name. Residents of Khademain and its surrounding usually bring their sick relative and tie them with his Tomb and ask for Allah for Shifa.

Tomb of Sayyid Murtadha A.R.

He was a great scholar and wrote many books and was the student of Sheikh Mufeed A.R.

Tomb of Sayyid Radhi A.R.

Sayyid Radhi A.R. compiled the sermons of Imam Ali A.S. and the collection is known as Nahjul Balagha. He too was the student of Sheikh Mufeed A.R.

Tomb of Sayyid Ismail Safrudin A.R.

He too was a great scholar and wrote many books.

Baghdad

Just over the bridge from the Holy City of Khademain lies
Baghdad. It is a modern city and all around it are many Mazaar of great scholars.

Masjid al-Buratha

This Masjid is between Khademain and Baghdad and it is a very famous Masjid.

It is narrated that this was a church before at the time of Imam Ali A.S. and when the Imam A.S. returned from the battle of Naherawan, the Christian priest invited our Imam to rest here, which he did for three days.

During his stay he saw the people of the church go out very far to fetch water and Imam Ali A.S. asked the priest why he does not dig a well in the church compound? The priest replied, that they tried but got salt water.

Imam Ali A.S. just hit the ground with his heel and water gushed out which was cold and sweet. There is a black stone at this miracle place. Also there is a white stone with Ayat-tul-Kursi written on it.

Mazaar of Hazrat Uthman Bin Saeed A.R.

He was the first Chief Duputy of our 12th Imam A.S. who used to be in contact with him. He was also a close companion of our 10th and 11th Imam A.S.

Mazaar of Hazrat Muhammad Bin Uthman A.R.

He was the son of Hazrat Uthman Bin Saeed and after his father passed away he took up the duties as the second Chief Deputy of our 12th Imam A.S.

Mazaar of Husayn Bin Rooh A.R.

He was the third deputy of our 12th Imam A.S.

Mazaar of Ali Bin Muhammad A.R.

He was the fourth and the last of the deputies of our 12th Imam A.S. He received a letter from our Imam telling him that there would be no more deputies after his death.

Mazaar Of Hazrat Qambar A.R.

During the time of Imam Ali A.S. he was a slave and the Imam bought him and freed him. Hazrat Qambar A.R. told Imam Ali A.S. that I will agree to be freed only if you promise me that as long as I live I will be living at your house and helping you and your family.

There is a famous story that one day Hazrat Qambar A.R. was sitting on a camel leading the caravan when a needy person came to Imam Ali A.S. and told him that he was very poor and asked the Imam to help him. Imam Ali A.S. told him to take the whole caravan of camels. On hearing this Hazrat Qambar A.R. jumped from the camel and when Imam Ali A.S. asked him why he did that, to which he replied he gave away the whole caravan to the needy person and as I was sitting on one of the camel that would have included me too.

Mazaar Of Hazrat Haafiz Muhammad Bin Yakub Al- Kulyani A.R.

He was a famous narrator of hadiths of the Prophet of Allah (SAW) and the Imams.

Marja at- Taqleed

You should visit Ayatullah al-Odhma Sayyid Ali Husayni Seestani his residence is just behind the Raudhah of Imam Ali A.S. and you will need to make an appointment. You can pay him Khums, Sadaqa, nadr and other huqooq money also medicine and used clothes for the poor and he will issue you a receipt with his seal and signature.

We hope that this booklet has been a help to you during your trip to 'Umra, Hajj and/or Ziyarat of the Fourteen Ma'soomeen and you are requested to remember all momineen and mominaat who have passed away and also those who are living in your prayers.
Mahmud & Zehra Habib
Organizer

Image:

SKETCH OF MASJID-E-SAHLAH.

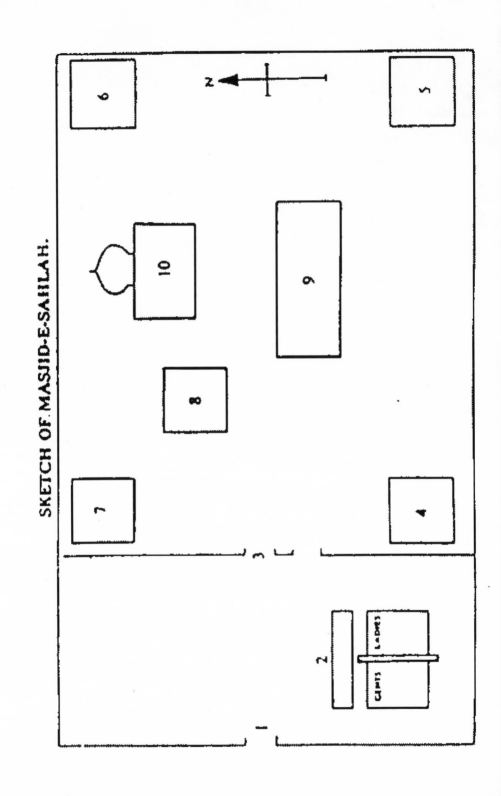

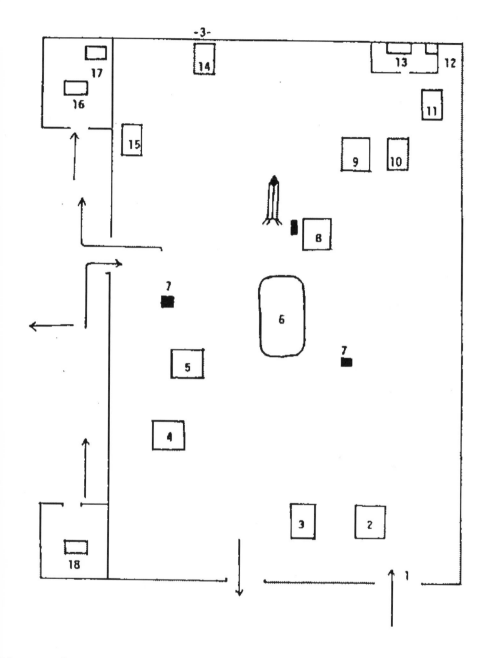

Shopping Guide in the Middle East

In the Middle East bargaining is customary and you should be able to bring down the price by 25 to 30% except for gold jewellery. The price of gold is almost the same through out the world except for labour cost. Jewelry manufactured in Shri Lanka will be cheaper than those manufactured in Saudi Arabia.

Saudi Arabia

Shopping for Musalla, Tasbih, Dates, Attar, Abaya, Scarves and jewelry and name brand watches.

In Jeddah: At the Balad which is the city center and all shopping malls are to be found here.

In Medina: Shops all around Masjid al-Nabawee. For exclusive items visit Quba Street near Masjid al-Quba.

In Makkah: Shops all around Masjid-ul-Haram for quality items visit shops in the Hilton Towers or go to Souk Azizia.

Damascus – Syria

You should pay a visit to the famous Souk Ahmadia which is adjacent to the Ommayad Mosque.

Iran

In Teheran: You should visit the shopping bazaar at the city center where you can buy anything you may think of, Saffron, Pistachios, Scarves, Abaya, woolen sweaters, you name it and they have got it.

In Mashad: The famous Bazaar al-Ridha' which is a walking distance from the Haram of Imam Ridha' A.S. All properties in this Bazaar is owned by the Trustees of Imam Ridha' A.S. All kinds of stones, like Aqeeq, Dure-Najaf, Firoza (Iran produces Firoza),Tasbih Maqhsood and Eerze Jawad Taawiz for children and rings for adults, Abaya Scarves, and Musallas with tasbih and Sajdagah.

In Mashad there is also another Bazaar called The Janatee Bazaar and here you can find exclusive items for ladies and gents wear including Abaya and scarves.

Iraq

In Najaf: Shopping stores just behind the Raudhah of Imam Ali A.S. where one can buy Sajdagah, Khak al-Shafa Tasbih, Feeroza, Aqeeq, Dur al-Najaf, Kafan, scarves and many more.

In Karbala': All around Imam Husayn A.S. Raudhah and Till al-Zainabia you can buy the same things that are also available in Najaf.

Source URL: https://www.al-islam.org/your-personal-guide-hajj-umrah-ziyarat-alha-
-mahmud-zehra-habib

Links
[1] https://www.al-islam.org/user/login?destination=node/15528%23comment-form
[2] https://www.al-islam.org/user/register?destination=node/15528%23comment-form
[3] https://www.al-islam.org/person/mahmud-zehra-habib
[4] https://www.al-islam.org/library/hajj-pilgrimage
[5] https://www.al-islam.org/tags/pilgrimage

[6] https://www.al-islam.org/tags/laws
[7] https://www.al-islam.org/tags/information
[8] mailto:devji@ican.net

Made in the USA
Coppell, TX
09 November 2022

86082076R00060